WHAT I BELIEVE

WHAT I BELIEVE

13 eminent people of our time argue
for their philosophy of life.

The Crossroad Publishing Company

© 1984 Waterstone and Company Limited,
edited by Mark Booth

Firethorn Press is an imprint of Waterstone and Company Limited.

First published 1984 in
The United States by
The Crossroad Publishing Company
370 Lexington Avenue
New York
NY 10017

First published in
Great Britain by
Waterstone and Company Limited.
193 Kensington High Street
London W8

Design and production in association with
Book Production Consultants, 47 Norfolk Street,
Cambridge.
Typeset by Cambridge Photosetting Services, 19–21 Sturton Street, Cambridge.
Printed and bound by Richard Clay PLC, Bungay, Suffolk

Library of Congress Catalog Card Number: 84-070838
ISBN (US): 0 8245 0676 6
ISBN (US): 0 8245 0677 4 (pbk)

ISBN (UK): 0 947752 02 1
ISBN (UK): 0 947752 03 X (pbk)

Contents

Acknowledgements

The editor and publisher wish to thank the following for their permission to reproduce copyright material:

W. H. Auden: Curtis Brown Ltd, for the Estate of W. H. Auden. Copyright © 1938 by W. H. Auden.

Albert Einstein: © The Hebrew University of Jerusalem (first published in 'I Believe', ed. Clifton Fadiman by Allen & Unwin UK and Simon & Schuster US).

Thomas Mann: © Alfred A. Knopf, Inc in the US (first published in 'Order of the Day: Political Essays and Speeches of Two Decades', by Alfred A. Knopf). © S. Fischer Verlag GmbH, Frankfurt am Main, in the UK.

Jacques Maritain: Eveline Garnier and Professor Olivier Lacombe.

Malcolm Muggeridge: William Collins & Sons Ltd in the UK (first published in 'Things Past', ed. Ian Hunter) and by William Morrow & Company in the US (first published in 'Things Past', ed. Ian Hunter). © 1966, 1978 Malcolm Muggeridge.

James Thurber: Hamish Hamilton Ltd in the UK (© the collection 1963 published by Hamish Hamilton, from Vintage Thurber Vols 1 and 2, by James Thurber, edited by Helen Thurber) and in the US Mrs James Thurber © 1939. From 'I Believe', published by Simon & Schuster.

Bertrand Russell: © The Bertrand Russell Estate.

H. G. Wells: © UK and US The Literary Executors of the Estate of H. G. Wells (first published in 'I Believe', ed. Clifton Fadiman in the UK by Allen & Unwin and in the US by Simon & Schuster).

Rebecca West: A. D. Peters & Co Ltd for © the Estate of Rebecca West.

Foreword

*W*hat are the most important questions you can ask yourself? What are your most sincere beliefs?

In *What I Believe* thirteen prominent people attempt a reasoned reply. A theologian, an evangelist, three philosophers, three novelists, a poet, an actor, a journalist, a humorist and a scientist, they find meaning and hope in a fascinating variety of areas of experience. Apart from their prominence in their respective fields, they perhaps have nothing in common except for their being unashamedly intellectual; with courage and with application they have tried to work out the right way to live. No account of human belief can be comprehensive – as W. H. Auden wrote, each individual's belief must be unique. But these revealing essays, which together form a sourcebook of the pioneering thought of our age, suggest the different types of beliefs that are open to us.

Theologian Jacques Maritain understands life as a process of education: 'To my way of thinking God, trains us through our disillusionments and mistakes, to understand at last that we must believe only in Him'. Similarly Thomas Mann sees life as a divinely inspired progress: 'it was to the end of her (nature's) own spiritualization that she brought man forth'. In his heart-felt piece Christian actor Martin Sheen puts more emphasis on man's active participation in the process: 'The direction of the universe can and will be determined by the presence of individual spirituality or the lack of it'. Evangelist Robert Schuller believes, further, that if we make a leap of faith, our participation becomes 'God directed and God guided'.

By comparison Albert Einstein finds consolation in what might be called the higher states of unbelief: 'To know that what is impenetrable to us really exists, manifesting itself as the highest wisdom and the most radiant beauty which our dull faculties can comprehend only in their most primitive forms – this knowledge, this feeling, is at the centre of true religiousness'. Instead of looking outward to the stars,

Bertrand Russell looks inward to the human heart to find value: 'No obedience to moral rules can take the place of love, and where love is genuine it will, if combined with intelligence, suffice to generate whatever moral rules are necessary'. His fellow humanist H. G. Wells, in his teasing, deceptively jaunty essay, seems to be approaching religious thought when he writes of the 'immortal soul of the race in which our own lives are like passing thoughts', the idea of which he believes is to be found 'in what Confucius called the Higher Person, in what St. Paul called the New Adam'.

James Thurber believes that, more than any other area of experience, art points us to what is most significant. He writes: 'Most of the faint intimations of immortality of which we are occasionally aware would seem to arise out of art'. On the other hand W. V. Quine, America's leading living philosopher, believes that science (which he epigrammatically defines as 'refined common sense') is the most life-enhancing area of human activity.

When society rather than the individual is under scrutiny, the tone of these testaments becomes caustic. Bertrand Russell suggests that: 'people wish to fight, and they therefore persuade themselves that it is to their interest to do so'. Rebecca West on the subject of strife contends that the 'subjection of women serves no purpose whatever except to gratify the desire for cruelty both in women and in men'. In W. H. Auden's view in 'the history of man, there have been a few civilized individuals but no civilized community, not one, ever'. The right-wing philosopher and polemicist, Antony Flew believes that socialists will cause further decline: 'how can any of us go on generously and politely conceding that those who still insist upon presenting and pursuing incomplete 'programmes for progress' are acting and talking in good faith, and with a single-minded devotion to human welfare?'

We can only hope with Malcolm Muggeridge that society's decline is necessary to throw into relief some version of the process of spiritual education of the individual, which is the cherished belief of people as diverse as Jacques Maritain, Thomas Mann, Robert Schuller and Martin Sheen: 'As human love only shines in all its splendour when the last tiny glimmer of desire has been extinguished, so we have to make the world a wilderness to find God'.

W. H. Auden

The most fêted English poet of the twentieth century and the greatest English-language poet after T. S. Eliot, W. H. Auden combined a brisk and entertaining style with a fundamental moral seriousness. The verbal fireworks of his poems are underpinned by an active concern with politics and religion. Often fiercely satirical and occasionally cruel, he tolerated no intellectual foolishness. His highly rational poetry shows a progressive refining of conscience, from the righteous anger of his early days to the quiet authority of the ageing philospher-poet.

Works include: 'The Orators', 'Look Stranger', 'Another Time', 'The Shield of Achilles', 'Homage to Clio' and 'Thank You, Fog'.

Everything that lives is Holy. – BLAKE

I

Goodness is easier to recognize than to define; only the greatest novelists can portray good people. For me, the least unsatisfactory description is to say that any thing or creature is good which is discharging its proper function, using its powers to the fullest extent permitted by its environment and its own nature – though we must remember that 'nature' and 'environment' are intellectual abstractions from a single, constantly changing reality. Thus, people are happy and good who have found their vocation: what vocations there are will depend upon the society within which they are practised.

There are two kinds of goodness, 'natural' and 'moral.' An organism is naturally good when it has reached a state of equilibrium with its environment. All healthy animals and plants are naturally good in this sense. But any change toward a greater freedom of action is a morally good change. I think it permissible, for example, to speak of a favourable mutation as a morally good act. But moral good passes into natural good. A change is made and a new equilibrium stabilized. Below man, this happens at once; for each species the change toward freedom is not repeated. In man, the evolution can be continued, each stage of moral freedom being superseded by a new one. For example, we frequently admire the 'goodness' of illiterate peasants as compared with the 'badness' of many townees. But this is a romantic confusion. The goodness we admire in the former is a natural, not a moral, goodness. Once, the life of a peasant represented the highest use of the powers of man, the farthest limit of his freedom of action. This is no longer true. The townee has a wider range of choice and fuller opportunities of using his power. He frequently chooses wrongly, and so becomes morally bad. We are right to condemn him for this, but to suggest that we should all return to the life of the peasant is to deny the possibility of moral progress. Worship of youth is another romantic pessimism of this kind.

(2) Similarly, there is natural and moral evil. Determined and unavoidable limits to freedom of choice and action, such as the

necessity for destroying life in order to eat and live, climate, accidents, are natural evils. If, on the other hand, I, say, as the keeper of a boarding-house, knowing that vitamins are necessary to health, continue, for reasons of gain or laziness, to feed my guests on an insufficient diet, I commit moral evil. Just as moral good tends to pass into natural good, so, conversely, what was natural evil tends, with every advance in knowledge, to become moral evil.

(3) The history of life on this planet is the history of the ways in which life has gained control over and freedom within its environment. Organisms may either adapt themselves to a particular environment – e.g. the fleshy leaves of the cactus permit it to live in a desert – or develop the means to change their environment – e.g. organs of locomotion.

Below the human level, this progress has taken place through structural biological changes, depending on the lack of mutations or the chances of natural selection. Only man, with his conscious intelligence, has been able to continue his evolution after his biological development has finished. By studying the laws of physical nature, he has gained a large measure of control over them and in so far as he is able to understand the laws of his own nature and of the societies in which he lives, he approaches that state where what he wills may be done. 'Freedom', as a famous definition has it, 'is consciousness of necessity.'

(4) The distinguishing mark of man as an animal is his plastic, unspecialized 'foetalized' nature. All other animals develop more quickly and petrify sooner. In other words, the dictatorship of heredity is weakest in man. He has the widest choice of environment, and, in return, changes in environment, either changes in nature or his social life, have the greatest effect on him.

(5) In contrast to his greatest rivals for biological supremacy, the insects, man has a specialized and concentrated central nervous system, and unspecialized peripheral organs, i.e. the stimuli he receives are collected and pooled in one organ. Intelligence and choice can only arise when more than one stimulus is presented at the same time in the same place.

(6) Man has always been a social animal living in communities. This falsifies any theories of Social Contract. The individual *in vacuo* is an intellectual abstraction. The individual is the product of social life; without it, he could be no more than a bundle of unconditioned reflexes. Men are born neither free nor good.

(7) Societies and cultures vary enormously. On the whole, Marx seems to me correct in his view that physical conditions and the forms of economic production have dictated the forms of communities: e.g. the geographical peculiarities of the Aegean peninsula produced small democratic city-states, while the civilizations based on river irrigation like Egypt and Mesopotamia were centralized autocratic empires.

(8) *But* we are each conscious of ourselves as a thinking, feeling, and willing whole, and this is the only whole of which we have direct knowledge. This experience conditions our thinking. I cannot see how other wholes, family, class, nation, etc., can be wholes to us except in a purely descriptive sense. We do not see a state, we see a number of individuals. Anthropological studies of different communities, such as Dr. Benedict's work on primitive American cultures, or that of the Lynds on contemporary Middletown, have shown the enormous power of a given cultural form to determine the nature of the individuals who live under it. A given cultural pattern develops those traits of character and modes of behaviour which it values, and suppresses those which it does not. But this does not warrant ascribing to a culture a super-personality, conscious of its parts as I can be conscious of my hand or liver. A society consists of a certain number of individuals living in a particular way in a particular place, at a particular time; nothing else.

(9) The distinction drawn by Locke between society and government is very important. Again, Marx seems to me correct in saying that sovereignty or government is not the result of a contract made by society as a whole, but has always been assumed by those people in society who owned the instruments of production.

Theories of Rights arise as a means to attack or justify a given social form, and are a sign of social strain. Burke, and later thinkers, who developed the idealist theory of the state, were correct in criticizing the *a priori* assumptions of Social Contract and in pointing out that society is a growing organism. But, by identifying society and government, they ignored the power of the latter to interfere with the natural growth of the former, and so were led to denying the right of societies to revolt against their governments, and to the hypostasization of the *status quo*.

(10) A favourite analogy for the state among idealist political thinkers is with the human body. This analogy is false. The constitution of the cells in the body is determined and fixed; nerve cells can only give rise to more nerve cells, muscle cells to muscle cells, etc. But,

in the transition from parent to child, the whole pack of inherited genetic characters is shuffled. The king's son may be a moron, the coal heaver's a mathematical genius. The entire pattern of talents and abilities is altered at every generation.

(11) Another false analogy is with the animal kingdom. Observed from the outside (how it appears to them no one knows), the individual animal seems to be sacrificed to the continuance of the species. This observation is used to deny the individual any rights against the state. But there is a fundamental difference between man and all other animals in that an animal which has reached maturity does not continue to evolve, but a man does. As far as we can judge, the only standard in the animal world is physical fitness, but in man a great many other factors are involved. What has survival value can never be determined; man has survived as a species through the efforts of individuals who at the time must often have seemed to possess very little biological survival value.

(12) Man's advance in control over his environment is making it more and more difficult for him, at least in the industrialized countries with a high standard of living, like America or England, to lead a naturally good life, and easier and easier to lead a morally bad one.

Let us suppose, for example, that it is sometimes good for mind and body to take a walk. Before there were means of mechanical transport, men walked because they could not do anything else; i.e. they committed naturally good acts. To-day, a man has to choose whether to use his car or walk. It is possible for him, by using the car on an occasion when he ought to walk, to commit a morally wrong act, and it is quite probable that he will.

II

(1) A society, then, is good in so far as

(*a*) it allows the widest possible range of choices to its members to follow those vocations to which they are suited;

(*b*) it is constantly developing, and providing new vocations which make a fuller demand upon their increasing powers.

The Greeks assumed that the life of intellectual contemplation was the only really 'good' vocation. It has become very much clearer now that this is only true for certain people, and that there are a great many other vocations of equal value: human nature is richer and more varied than the Greeks thought.

(2) No society can be absolutely good. Utopias, whether like Aldous Huxley's Brave New World or Dante's Paradiso, because they are static, only portray states of natural evil or good. (Someone, I think it was Landor, said of the characters in the *Inferno*: "But they don't want to get out.") People committing acts in obedience to law or habit are not being moral. As voluntary action always turns, with repetition, into habit, morality is only possible in a world which is constantly changing and presenting a fresh series of choices. No society is absolutely good; but some are better than others.

(3) If we look at a community at any given moment, we see that it consists of good men and bad men, clever men and stupid men, sensitive and insensitive, law-abiding and lawless, rich and poor. Our politics, our view of what form our society and our government should take here and now, will depend on

(*a*) how far we think the bad is due to preventable causes;

(*b*) what, if we think the causes preventable, we find them to be. If we take the extremely pessimistic view that evil is in no way preventable, our only course is the hermit's, to retire altogether from this wicked world. If we take a fairly pessimistic view, that badness is inherited (i.e. that goodness and badness are not determined by social relations), we shall try to establish an authoritarian regime of the good. If, on the other hand, we are fairly optimistic, believing that bad environment is the chief cause of badness in individuals, and that the environment can be changed, we shall tend toward a belief in some sort of democracy. Personally I am fairly optimistic, partly for reasons which I have tried to outline above, and partly because the practical results of those who have taken the more pessimistic view do not encourage me to believe that they are right.

(4) *Fairly* optimistic. In the history of man, there have been a few civilized individuals but no civilized community, not one, ever. Those who talk glibly of Our Great Civilization, whether European, American, Chinese, or Russian, are doing their countries the greatest disservice. We are still barbarians. All advances in knowledge, from Galileo down to Freud or Marx, are, in the first impact, humiliating; they begin by showing us that we are not as free or as grand or as good as we thought; and it is only when we realize this that we can begin to study how to overcome our own weakness.

(5) What then are the factors which limit and hinder men from developing their powers and pursuing suitable vocations?

(*a*) Lack of material goods. Man is an animal and until his immediate material and economic needs are satisfied, he cannot develop further. In the past this has been a natural evil: methods of production and distribution were too primitive to guarantee a proper standard of life for everybody. It is doubtful whether this is any longer true; in which case, it is a moral and remediable evil. Under this head I include all questions of wages, food, housing, health, insurance, etc.

(*b*) Lack of education. Unless an individual is free to obtain the fullest education with which his society can provide him, he is being injured by society. This does not mean that everybody should have the *same* kind of education, though it does mean, I think, education of some kind or other, up to university age. Education in a democracy must have two aims. It must give vocational guidance and training; assist each individual to find out where his talents lie, and then help him to develop these to the full – this for some people might be completed by sixteen – and it must also provide a general education; develop the reason and the consciousness of every individual, whatever his job, to a point where he can for himself distinguish good from bad, and truth from falsehood – this requires a much longer educational period.

At present education is in a very primitive stage; we probably teach the wrong things to the wrong people at the wrong time. It is dominated, at least in England, by an academic tradition which, except for the specially gifted, only fits its pupils to be schoolteachers. It is possible that the time for specialization (i.e. vocational training) should be in early adolescence, the twelve-to-sixteen group, and again in the latter half of the university period; but that the sixteen-to-twenty age group should have a general education.

(*c*) Lack of occupations which really demand the full exercise of the individual's powers. This seems to me a very difficult problem indeed. The vast majority of jobs in a modern community do people harm. Children admire gangsters more than they admire factory operatives because they sense that being a gangster makes more demands on the personality than being a factory operative and is therefore, for the individual, morally better. It isn't that the morally better jobs are necessarily better rewarded economically: for instance, my acquaintance with carpenters leads me to think carpentry a very good profession, and my acquaintance with stockbrokers to think stockbroking a very bad one. The only jobs known to me which seem worthy of respect, both from the point of view of the individual and society, are being a creative artist, some kind of highly skilled craftsman, a research scientist, a doctor, a teacher, or a farmer. This difficulty runs far deeper than our present knowledge or any immediate political change we can imagine, and is therefore still, to a certain extent, a natural rather than a moral evil, though it is obviously much aggravated by gross inequalities in economic reward, which could be remedied. I don't myself much like priggish phrases such as 'the right use of leisure.' I agree with Eric Gill that work is what one does to please oneself, leisure the time one has to serve the community. The most one can say is that we must never forget that most people are being degraded by the work they do, and that the possibilities of sharing the duller jobs through the whole community will have to be explored much more fully. Incidentally, there is reason for thinking that the routine manual and machine-minding jobs are better tolerated by those whose talents are for book learning than by those whose talents run in the direction of manual skill.

(*d*) Lack of suitable psychological conditions. People cannot grow unless they are happy and, even when their material needs have been satisfied, they still need many other things. They want to be liked and to like other people; to feel valuable, both in their own eyes and in the eyes of others; to feel free and to feel responsible; above all, not to feel lonely and isolated. The first great obstacle is the size of modern communities. By nature, man seems adapted to live in communities of a very moderate size; his economic life has compelled him to live in ever-enlarging ones. Many of the damaging effects of family life described by modern psychologists may be the result of our attempt to make the family group satisfy psychological needs which can only be satisfied by the community group. The family is based on inequality, the parent-child relationship; the community is, or should be, based on equality, the relationship of free citizens. We need both. Fortunately, technical advances, such as cheap electrical power, are making smaller social units more of a practical possibility than they seemed fifty years ago, and people with as divergent political views as the anarchists and industrialists can agree about the benefits of industrial decentralization.

The second obstacle is social injustice and inequality. A man cannot be a happy member of a community if he feels that the community is treating him unjustly; the more complicated and impersonal economic life becomes, the truer this is. In a small factory where employer and employees know each other personally, i.e. where the conditions approximate those of family life, the employees will accept without resentment a great deal more inequality than their fellows in a modern large-scale production plant.

III

Society consists of a number of individual wills living in association. There is no such thing as a general will of society, except in so far as all these individual wills agree in desiring certain material things, e.g. food and clothes. It is also true, perhaps, that all desire happiness and goodness, but their conceptions of these may and do conflict with each other. Ideally, government is the means by which all the individual wills are assured complete freedom of moral choice and at the same time prevented from ever clashing. Such an ideal government, of course, does not and could not ever exist. It presupposes that every individual in society possesses equal power, and also that every individual takes part in the government.

(2) In practice, the majority is always ruled by a minority, a certain number of individuals who decide what a law shall be, and who command enough force to see that the majority obeys them. To do this, they must also command a varying degree of consent by the majority, though this consent need not be and never is complete. They must, for example, have the consent of the armed forces and the police, and they must either control the financial resources of society, or have the support of those who do.

(3) Democracy assumes, I think correctly, the right of every individual to revolt against his government by voting against it. It has not been as successful as its advocates hoped, firstly, because it failed to realize the pressure that the more powerful and better educated classes could bring to bear upon the less powerful and less educated in their decisions – it ignored the fact that in an economically unequal society votes may be equal but voters are not – and secondly, because it assumed, I think quite wrongly, that voters living in the same geographical area would have the same interests, again ignoring economic differences and the change from an agricultural to an industrial economy. I believe that representation should be by trade or profession. No one person has exactly the same interests as another; but I, say, as a writer in Birmingham, have more interests in common with other writers in Leeds or London than I have with my next-door neighbour who manufactures cheap jewellery. This failure of the geographical unit to correspond to a genuine political unit is one of

the factors responsible for the rise of the party machine. We rarely elect a local man whom we know personally; we have to choose one out of two or three persons offered from above. This seems to me thoroughly unsatisfactory. I think one of our mistakes is that we do not have enough stages in election; a hundred thousand voters are reduced by a single act to one man who goes to Parliament. This must inevitably mean a large degree of dictatorship from above. A sane democracy would, I feel, choose its representatives by a series of electoral stages, each lower stage electing the one above it.

(4) Legislation is a form of coercion, of limiting freedom. Coercion is necessary because societies are not free communities; we do not choose the society into which we are born; we can attempt to change it, but we cannot leave it. Ideally, people should be free to know evil and to choose the good, but the consequences of choosing evil are often to compel others to do evil. The guiding principle of legislation in a democracy should be, not to make people good, but to prevent them making each other bad against their will. Thus we all agree that there should be laws against theft or murder, because no one chooses to be stolen from or murdered. But it is not always so simple. It is argued by *laissez-faire* economists that legislation concerning hours of work, wages, etc., violates the right of the individual wills to bargain freely. But this presupposes that the bargaining powers of different wills are equal, and that each bargain is an individual act. Neither of these assumptions is true, and economic legislation is justified because they are not.

But there are other forms of legislation which are less justified. It is true that the individual will operating in a series of isolated acts is an abstraction – our present acts are the product of past acts and in their turn determine future ones – but I think the law has to behave as if this abstraction were a fact, otherwise there is no end to legislative interference. Take the case, for instance, of drink. If I become a drunkard, I may not only impair my own health, but also that of my children; and it can be argued, and often is, that the law should see that I do not become one by preventing me from purchasing alcohol. I think, however, that this is an unjustifiable extension of the law's function. Everything I do, the hour I go to bed, the literature I read, the temperature at which I take my bath, affects my character for good or bad, and so, ultimately, the characters of those with whom I come in contact. If the legislator is once allowed to consider the distant effects of my acts, there is no reason why he should not decide everything for me. The law has to limit itself to considering the act in isolation: if the act directly violates the will of another, the law is justified in interfering; if only indirectly, it is not. Nearly all legislation on 'moral' matters, such as drink, gambling, sexual behaviour between adults, etc., seems to me bad.

(5) In theory, every individual has a right to his own conception of what form society ought to take and what form of government there should be and to exercise his will to realize it; on the other hand, everyone else has a right to reject his conception. In practice, this boils down to the right of different political parties to exist, parties representing the main divisions of interest in society. As the different sectional interests cannot form societies on their own – e.g. the employees cannot set up one state by themselves and the employers another – there is always coercion of the weaker by the stronger by propaganda, legislation, and sometimes physical violence; and the more evenly balanced the opposing forces are, the more violent that coercion is likely to become.

I do not see how in politics one can decide *a priori* what conduct is moral, or what degree of tolerance there should be. One can only decide which party in one's private judgment has the best view of what society ought to be, and to support it; and remember that, since all coercion is a moral evil, we should view with extreme suspicion those who welcome it.

Intolerance is an evil and has evil consequences we can never accurately foresee and for which we shall always have to suffer; but there are occasions on which we must be prepared to accept the responsibility of our convictions. We must be as tolerant as we dare – only the future can judge whether we were tyrants or foolishly weak – and if we cannot dare very far, it is a serious criticism of ourselves and our age.

(6) But we do have to choose, every one of us. We have the misfortune or the good luck to be living in one of the great critical historical periods, when the whole structure of our society and its cultural and metaphysical values are undergoing a radical change. It has happened before, when the Roman Empire collapsed, and at the Reformation, and it may happen again in the future.

In periods of steady evolution, it is possible for the common man to pursue his private life without bothering his head very much over the principles and assumptions by which he lives, and to leave politics in the hands of professionals. But ours is not such an age. It is idle to lament that the world is becoming divided into hostile ideological camps; the division is a fact. No policy of isolation is possible. Democracy, liberty, justice, and reason are being seriously threatened and, in many parts of the world, destroyed. It is the duty of every one of us, not only to ourselves but to future generations of men, to have a clear understanding of what we mean when we use these words, to remember that while an idea can be absolutely bad, a person can never be, and to defend what we believe to be right, perhaps even at the cost of our lives and those of others.

Albert Einstein

The most influential physicist since Newton, Albert Einstein brought about a scientific revolution which has completely changed our ideas of space and time. His deeply intuitive approach to science was integrated into a consistent philosophy of life: "Science without religion is lame," he argued, "religion without science is blind." In Einstein's view the mysterious is the source of all that is most beautiful and creative in life, whether in science, religion or art.

Works include: 'Investigations on the Theory of the Brownian Movement', 'The Evolution of Physics' and 'Relativity: the Special and General Theory'.

S trange is our situation here upon earth. Each of us comes for a short visit, not knowing why, yet sometimes seeming to divine a purpose.

From the standpoint of daily life, however, there is one thing we do know: that man is here for the sake of other men – above all for those upon whose smile and well-being our own happiness depends, and also for the countless unknown souls with whose fate we are connected by a bond of sympathy. Many times a day I realize how much my own outer and inner life is built upon the labours of my fellow-men, both living and dead, and how earnestly I must exert myself in order to give in return as much as I have received. My peace of mind is often troubled by the depressing sense that I have borrowed too heavily from the work of other men.

I do not believe we can have any freedom at all in the philosophical sense, for we act not only under external compulsion but also by inner necessity. Schopenhauer's saying – "A man can surely do what he wills to do, but he cannot determine what he wills" – impressed itself upon me in youth and has always consoled me when I have witnessed or suffered life's hardships. This conviction is a perpetual breeder of tolerance, for it does not allow us to take ourselves or others too seriously; it makes rather for a sense of humour.

To ponder interminably over the reason for one's own existence or the meaning of life in general seems to me, from an objective point of view, to be sheer folly. And yet everyone holds certain ideals by which he guides his aspiration and his judgment. The ideals which have always shone before me and filled me with the joy of living are goodness, beauty, and truth. To make a goal of comfort or happiness has never appealed to me; a system of ethics built on this basis would be sufficient only for a herd of cattle.

Without the sense of collaborating with like-minded beings in the pursuit of the ever unattainable in art and scientific research, my life would have been empty. Ever since childhood I have scorned the commonplace limits so often set upon human ambition. Possession, outward success, publicity, luxury – to me these have always been contemptible. I believe that a simple and unassuming manner of life is best for everyone, best both for the body and the mind.

My passionate interest in social justice and social responsibility has always stood in curious contrast to a marked lack of desire for direct association with men and women. I am a horse for single harness, not cut out for tandem or team work. I have never belonged wholeheartedly to country or state, to my circle of friends, or even to my own family. These ties have always been accompanied by a vague aloofness, and the wish to withdraw into myself increases with the years.

Such isolation is sometimes bitter, but I do not regret being cut off from the understanding and sympathy of other men. I lose something by it, to be sure, but I am compensated for it in being rendered independent of the customs, opinions, and prejudices of others, and am not tempted to rest my peace of mind upon such shifting foundations.

My political ideal is democracy. Everyone should be respected as an individual, but no one idolized. It is an irony of fate that I should have been showered with so much uncalled-for and unmerited admiration and esteem. Perhaps this adulation springs from the unfulfilled wish of the multitude to comprehend the few ideas which I, with my weak powers, have advanced.

Full well do I know that in order to attain any definite goal it is imperative that *one* person should do the thinking and commanding and carry most of the responsibility. But those who are led should not be driven, and they should be allowed to choose their leader. It seems to me that the distinctions separating the social classes are false; in the last analysis they rest on force. I am convinced that degeneracy follows every autocratic system of violence, for violence inevitably attracts moral inferiors. Time has proved that illustrious tyrants are succeeded by scoundrels.

For this reason I have always been passionately opposed to such regimes as exist in Russia. The thing which has discredited the European forms of democracy is not the basic theory of democracy itself, which some say is at fault, but the instability of our political leadership, as well as the impersonal character of party alignments.

What is truly valuable in our bustle of life is not the nation, I should say, but the creative and impressionable individuality, the personality

– he who produces the noble and sublime while the common herd remains dull in thought and insensible in feeling.

This subjct brings me to that vilest offspring of the herd mind – the odious militia. The man who enjoys marching in line and file to the strains of music falls below my contempt; he received his great brain by mistake – the spinal cord would have been amply sufficient. Heroism at command, senseless violence, the accursed bombast of patriotism – how intensely I despise them! War is low and despicable, and I had rather be smitten to shreds than participate in such doings.

Any such stain on humanity should be erased without delay. I think well enough of human nature to believe that it would have been wiped out long ago had not the common sense of nations been systematically corrupted through school and press for business and political reasons.

The most beautiful thing we can experience is the mysterious. It is the source of all true art and science. He to whom this emotion is a stranger, who can no longer pause to wonder and stand rapt in awe, is as good as dead: his eyes are closed. This insight into the mystery of life, coupled though it be with fear, has also given rise to religion. To know that what is impenetrable to us really exists, manifesting itself as the highest wisdom and the most radiant beauty which our dull faculties can comprehend only in their most primitive forms – this knowledge, this feeling, is at the centre of true religiousness. In this sense, and in this sense only, I belong in the ranks of devoutly religious men.

I cannot imagine a God who rewards and punishes the objects of his creation, whose purposes are modelled after our own – a God, in short, who is but a reflection of human frailty. Neither can I believe that the individual survives the death of his body, although feeble souls harbour such thoughts through fear or ridiculous egotism. It is enough for me to contemplate the mystery of conscious life perpetrating itself through all eternity, to reflect upon the marvellous structure of the universe which we can dimly perceive, and to try humbly to comprehend even an infinitesimal part of the intelligence manifested in nature.

Antony Flew

A ntony Flew is one of the most stimulating and combative philosophers writing in English today. He has taken on the mantle of Bertrand Russell as the foremost popularizer of philosophical ideas, his 'Introduction to Western Philosophy' having become the standard alternative to Russell's 'History of Western Philosophy'. Moreover his controversial involvement with the Freedom Association and the Voluntary Euthanasia Society puts him in the vanguard of the new movement to bring the powers of the philosopher to bear on current issues in politics and personal ethics.

Works include: 'Hume's Philosophy of Belief', 'God and Philosophy', 'Introduction to Western Philosophy' and 'Thinking about Thinking'.

Asked to say 'What I believe' a professional philosopher has to start from what one of the greatest of us, Immanuel Kant, once distinguished as the three chief questions of metaphysics – God, freedom, and immortality. To the first and to the third my response has been throughout the whole of my adult life consistently negative; while to the second it has been equally consistently, even passionately, positive. What has changed over the years has been some of the supporting arguments and, in the case of freedom, my beliefs about the metaphysical implications.

As a son of the manse I naturally began by accepting that the burden of proof must lie not with the proposers but the opposers; it being up to me to offer sufficient reason for rejecting the faith of my parents.

To come to see that this is wrong was a major advance. For the truth is that it must be incumbent upon anyone maintaining that there is some super Something or Someone, somehow behind and additional to the whole observable Universe, to try to justify their confidence that this is so; and, still more, their confidence that they themselves possess some knowledge about the nature of that Something or that Someone. On this topic so many radically different views have been and are held by otherwise reasonable, serious, concerned, and competent people that no one has any business to maintain any one of these views without first attending to a deal of argument both for and against their own favoured position.

A second major advance is one, it seems, made even less often than the first. This consists in recognizing that any truly adequate apologetic for any such position must begin from the beginning. Both because of the vast variety of different conceptions of God which have been and still are on offer, and because the attributes postulated are so extraordinary as well as in some cases seemingly incompatible one with another, it is essential for any apologist to begin by expounding his own idea of God and by trying to show that this idea is coherent.

31

Only when and if these preliminary tasks have been satisfactorily performed can we go on to ask whether the concept thus established does in fact have application; whether, that is, God, so conceived, does in fact exist. What reasons are there for believing this?

At this stage somebody will want to tell us that of course everybody knows that it is not possible either to prove or to disprove the existence of God; and hence that this kind of question belongs to the province of faith, not reason. Any such wiseacre contention is doubly misguided. In a matter of what all are agreed is of supreme importance it is quite breathtakingly frivolous to plump, by taking a blind leap of faith, for any one particular position without having any sort of good reason for leaping in that direction or even for leaping at all. Furthermore, in the days before the Second Vatican Council, when Roman Catholics *were* Roman Catholics, all those well instructed in that faith knew that anyone daring to challenge its categorical claim: "that the one and true God our creator and Lord can be known through the creation by the natural light of reason" would be anathematized.

If we do allow it to be in principle impossible to know whether or not some suggested conception of God does in fact have application, then this carries the most damaging implications. For how can any such concession be reconciled with the assumption that that conception's sponsors know what they are saying? What is it that their assertion that their God exists is asserting to be the case? The simple yet surely sufficient reason why I do not myself believe in God is that I have never yet encountered any truly systematic and comprehensive apologetic; an apologetic, that is, which, after first expounding and defending its preferred conception, then proceeds to provide adequate, evidencing reasons for believing that that conception does indeed have application.

Consider next doctrines of human immortality. Here we face an enormous initial obstacle. This consists in all the familiar, undeniable facts epitomized in that pet major premise of the traditional formal logic: "All men are mortal". There appear to be three, but only three, directions in which we might hope to find a way around this obstacle. First, it is suggested that a tenuous and elusive 'astral body' detaches itself at death, and that this is the essential person which survives, whether for a limited time or for ever. There is, however, no respectable evidence for this hypothesis. It escapes decisive falsification only by egregiously arbitrary postulations: there is, perhaps, some fresh and presently undetectable sort of stuff of which 'astral bodies' are conveniently composed; and so on.

Second, it is suggested that the flesh and blood person may eventually be, by an act of sheer Omnipotence, reconstituted. In 'The Night Journey' in the *Koran*, for example, unbelievers ask: "When we are turned to bones and dust, shall we be raised to life?" The Prophet there answers with a question: "Do they not see that Allah, who has created the heavens and the earth, has power to create their like?" To this the contemporary unbeliever should reply that it would indeed be no more than *their like*; re-creations would be replicas, not the authentic originals.

The third and by far the most popular suggestion is that the real or essential person is a more or less temporary, incorporeal occupant of the body. Such a being could presumably escape at death, undetected and indeed undetectable. Could it not then survive indefinitely without occupying any space, despite possessing – perhaps – positions? The formidable difficulties of any such Platonic-Cartesian account of the nature of man have only fairly recently begun to be recognized. It is because I believe these to be insurmountable that I can find no warrant for challenging the common sense conviction that when we are dead, we are dead; and that that is – necessarily – final.

Here it must suffice to insist that all the words for person cannot but be explained and ostensively defined by reference to specimens of that class of flesh and blood creatures to which we all belong. Anyone, therefore, who wants to identify us with hypothesized incorporeal entities is going to have their work cut out. Nor will it be easy to make a real distinction between incorporeal people, whether human or Divine, and no people at all.

Suppose that, in desperation, it is proposed that these hypothesized entities must be nothing but collections of moments of consciousness; identifiable, if at all, only by themselves. Then we have to reflect that David Hume, who held that this is what in some understanding persons actually are, eventually allowed that he was at a loss to specify either the uniting bond by which one such collection might be distinguished from another; or how one and the same collection could even by itself be, after an interval, reidentified. Nor should we too comfortably concede that it makes any sense at all to speak of moments of consciousness occurring altogether independently, without being the adjectival experiences of any sort of substantival subject. None of Hume's successors have to my knowledge excogitated any more satisfactory answers to these intractable problems than Hume's admittedly abortive attempts.

Freedom is easier. Here the first, too rarely taken, step is to realize that the great questions are about the reality not of freewill but of action, and about what this implies, both to those who act of their own freewill and to those who, by contrast, act under compulsion. Anyone who is in any direction an agent necessarily has some choice, although, precisely in virtue of having that choice, they cannot choose not to choose.

There is, therefore, a world of difference: between those who receive from *The Godfather* 'offers which they cannot refuse'; and the errant Mafioso gunned down from behind. The former are agents, who in some profound sense, could have done otherwise; however unreasonable it might have been either to predict that they would or to require that they should. The latter, in that very moment of sudden death, ceases to be.

To elucidate that profound sense, and to discover what action does and does not presuppose and imply, we can turn to the much underappreciated chapter 'Of Power' in John Locke's *Essay concerning Human Understanding*. 'Every one', he contends, 'finds in himself a power to begin or forbear, continue or put an end to several actions. . . . From the consideration of the extent of this power . . . which everyone finds in himself, arise the ideas of liberty and necessity.' Except that Locke should surely have said not 'liberty' but 'agency,' these two sentences embrace the whole heart of the matter.

He goes on to offer, in effect, ostensive definitions of the two contrasting key terms: 'We have instances enough, and often more than enough, in our own bodies. A man's heart beats, and the blood circulates, which it is not in his power . . . to stop; and therefore in respect of these motions, where rest depends not on his choice . . . he is not . . . [an] agent. Convulsive actions agitate his legs, so that though he wills it never so much he cannot . . . stop their motion (as in that odd disease called *Chorea Sancti Viti*) but he is perpetually dancing. He is . . . under as much necessity of moving as a stone that falls, or a tennis-ball struck with a racket.'

The two key terms thus can be, and surely cannot but be, defined ostensively. It therefore follows that there is no room for any denials either that there are, or that we know that there are, plenty of occasions upon which they can be correctly and truly applied. Nor, for the same reason, is there any room to maintain that, *ultimately* or *really*, all chosen courses of action are physically necessitated; like 'a stone that falls, or a tennis-ball struck with a racket.'

It cannot be so, not even *ultimately* or *really*, since this sort of physical or factual necessity has been defined, and could only have been defined, ostensively and by reference to the contrast with choice and the possibility of doing otherwise – two essential characteristics of (human) agency. Note also that, when and in so far as the notion of cause contains this idea of necessity, human actions have to possess what some have thought the distinctively Divine property of being uncaused causes!

Anyone aspiring to refute this crucial cluster of contentions about choice and about this sort of necessity is invited to develop their own alternative explanation of the meanings of the key terms. To do the job it has to be an explanation which could be understood by creatures which were not themselves agents, limited by such necessities and impossibilities. It also has to be an explanation making no ostensive mention of actual instances either of choice or of these necessities and impossibilities. The aspiring refuters are most welcome to try: I wish them the best of British luck.

So much for my fundamental beliefs about what *is* the case. As to what I believe *ought* to be, I believe that there ought to be more freedom and less compulsion, more satisfaction and less suffering, more rationality and realism and less irrationality and unrealism. Commitment to these three values has led me into various pressure-group activities, and has in large part determined the subject area of my books and articles.

Thus it was primarily a concern for individual liberty which led to my involvement in the Homosexual Law Reform Society, the Abortion Law Reform Association, and the Voluntary Euthanasia Society. I have always wanted to see all our laws constrained by the principles so happily stated in the 1945 Kemalist constitution of Turkey: 'Every Turk is born free and lives free. He has liberty to do anything which does not harm other persons. The natural right of the individual to liberty is limited only by the liberties enjoyed by his fellow citizens.'

In the case of the first two of these three pressure-groups my own activities have been pretty modest. But I have long since lost count of those many meetings before which I have argued the case for legalizing voluntary euthanasia, and for several years I served on the Executive Committee of the VES. It was indeed during my three-year stint as Chairman of that EC, and on my initiative, that the Society decided to produce its D-I-Y *Guide to Self-Deliverance*. This decision had the effects – along with some others less welcome – of winning enormous and unprecedented publicity for our cause as well as generating an explosive increase in the membership of our Society.

Again, it was my commitment to rationality and to a would-be unblinkered realism which led me into the Rationalist Press Association. This, like my first joinings of all the other three pressure-groups aforementioned, was way back in the early fifties, after the RPA had undertaken to publish my first book – the ill-written and ill-starred *New Approach to Psychical Research*. The same concerns led me to write *God and Philosophy* and *The Presumption of Atheism* (both about to be reissued under fresh titles in the USA), as well as to edit *Body, Mind and Death*.

But in these cases there was a second motive also, arising from the second of my three main values: that there ought to be more satisfaction and less suffering. For, in their Roman Catholic forms, the religious doctrines against which I argued constitute the chief rational basis for opposition to effective population control. I have myself since my undergraduate days and earlier been an utterly convinced, strenuously propagandizing Neo-Malthusian.

Certainly there are many faults in the theorizing of Malthus. His preferred policy proposals too are open to objection on several counts. But one truth is by now inescapable; or should be. This the classical economist William Nassau Senior offered as the main gain from his own long controversy with Malthus. 'No plan for social improvement can be complete', Senior wrote, 'unless it embraces the means both of increasing production, and of preventing population making proportionate advance.'

Such lamentably incomplete plans continue to be presented, although fewer perhaps now than ten or twenty years ago. Most importantly the Chinese Communists have at last, and at least in this, jettisoned the bigoted teachings of Marx and Engels. How sad for their subjects – a quarter of all the world's people – that in those first thirty wasted years those uncriticisable and irremovable rulers allowed the demographic situation so to deteriorate that there is now no alternative to their present policies, appallingly drastic and demanding though these are. As for the rest, how can any of us go on generously and politely conceding that those who still insist upon presenting and pursuing incomplete 'programmes for progress' are acting and talking in good faith, and with a singleminded devotion to human welfare?

The last ten years have been a period both of renewed Marxist-Leninist advance on the international stage and of the transforming degeneration of the Labour Party in Britain into a Benno-Bolshevik front organization. In reaction my own spare time activism has become more and more concentrated onto the fight against socialism. This is a fight in which, as I see it, all my three main values demand that I engage. That is why I became a founder member of the Council of the Freedom Association, of the Academic Advisory Board of the Adam Smith Institute, and of two of the specialist groups of the Centre for Policy Studies.

The concern for rationality and for unblinkered realism is engaged because in these days, now that so many countries have suffered so much from socialism in practice, advocates understandably find it hard to sustain their advocacy without irrationality and without either misrepresenting or ignoring the unlovely realities involved in the fulfilment of their ideas. I am the more confident in this perhaps aggressively dogmatic conclusion inasmuch as I have reached it only slowly and laboriously: I was for many years myself strongly socialist, being saved from a spell in the Communist Party only by the shock of seeing the great, international, anti-facist struggle suddenly, after the 1939 German-Soviet Pact, transformed by Stalin's dictate into an imperialist war.

The classical Utilitarian concern to increase satisfaction and reduce suffering is engaged because monopoly socialism is such an inefficient way of producing what consumers want at the lowest possible price. Its rival, pluralistic capitalism, gives all actual and potential competitors an individual interest in doing precisely that. Consider, for instance, the fact that all the public sector unions in Britain are unanimously and often even violently opposed to the introduction of competition, whether by putting operations out to tender or otherwise. Why?

Certainly almost if not quite all the officials of these as of other British unions are socialists. So if they, who are in a better position than the rest of us to know, really believed that direct labour was in fact producing the best possible goods and services at the lowest possible price, how could they fail to welcome all these still much too few and half-hearted moves as a superb opportunity to demonstrate the superiority of socialism?' How else can we construe their 'total opposition' save as a tacit confession that they – they who, we must emphasize again, are in an excellent position to know – do indeed know that overmanning, restrictive practices, and all other forms of inefficiency and exploitation are endemic in the monopoly, direct labour situation? That and that alone must be the true reason why these trades union and bureaucratic monopolists, like all monopolists, fight to preserve their prescriptive rights thus to exploit the rest of us.

Finally, there is the concern for liberty. I am persuaded that a predominantly private and pluralist economy is a necessary, although of course not a sufficient, condition for the maintenance of the fundamental liberties of a free and pluralist political society. This is a main thesis of F. A. Hayek's *The Road to Serfdom*, a work which when it first came out in 1944 I was not sufficiently openminded to address. It is a thesis which has been widely accepted. Its compelling force is in a devious fashion recognized by many who would profess to be still socialists and democrats. These slithy toves, choosing to misrepresent it as a silly claim not about a necessary but a sufficient condition, respond with some knee-jerk sneer against Chile, or possibly Taiwan or South Korea.

Our most powerful and persuasive endorsement comes, however, from the ideological citadel of by far the most powerful and persistent of all enemies of liberty. In 1971, with its eyes then most immediately on Chile and France, the Institute of Marxism-Leninism in Moscow sketched a programme for achieving, through 'United Front' or 'Broad Left' tactics, irreversible Communist domination: 'Having once acquired political power, the working class implements the liquidation of the private ownership of the means of production. . . . As a result, under socialism, there remains no ground for the existence of any opposition parties counter-balancing the Communist Party.'

Wise readers will take note that the future one-party monopolists do not have to be called, or to have been from the beginning organized as, a Communist Party.

Thomas Mann

The major German novelist of the twentieth century, Thomas Mann upheld the spiritual tradition of Wagner, Schopenhauer and Nietzsche against the brutal political ideas that have marred the epoch. His largely autobiographical novels narrate the progress of a sensitive artist through the upheavals of the age, exploring the spirituality latent in politics and the political implications of the spiritual. As an artist he felt himself not entitled to the comforts of an ordinary social life, and so became the epitome of the tortured twentieth-century intellectual.

Works include: 'Buddenbrooks', 'Death in Venice', 'The Magic Mountain', 'Joseph and his brothers' and 'Doctor Faustus'.

I find it singularly difficult to formulate, either briefly or in a more extended pronouncement, my philosophical ideas or convictions – shall I say my views, or, even better, my feelings? – about life and the world. The habit of expressing indirectly, through the media of picture and rhythm, my attitude toward the world and the problem of existence, is not conducive to abstract exposition. Summoned to speak, as now, I seem to myself a little like Faust, when Gretchen asks him how he stands about religion.

You certainly do not mean to put me through my catechism, but in practice your inquiry comes to much the same thing. For truly I find it almost easier – in my position – to say how I feel about religion than about philosophy. I do, indeed, disclaim any doctrinaire attitude in spiritual matters. The ease with which some people let the word God fall from their lips – or even more extraordinarily from their pens – is always a great astonishment to me. A certain modesty, even embarrassment, in things of religion is clearly more fitting to me and my kind than any posture of bold self-confidence. It seems that only by indirection can we approach the subject: by the parable, the ethical symbolism wherein, if I may so express myself, the concept becomes secularized, is temporarily divested of its priestly garment and contents itself with the humanly spiritual.

I read lately in a treatise by a learned friend something about the origin and history of the Latin word *religio*. The verb *relegere* or *religare* from which it is thought to derive means originally in its profane sense to take care, to pay heed, to bethink oneself. As the opposite of *neglegere* (neglect, *negligere*) it means an attentive, concerned and careful, conscientious, cautious attitude – the opposite, as I said, of all carelessness and negligence. And the word *religio* seems to have retained throughout the Latin age this sense of consciousness, of conscientious scruples. It is thus used, without necessary reference to religious, godly matters, in the very oldest Latin literature.

I was glad to hear all that. Well, I said to myself, if that is being religious, then every artist, simply in his character as artist, may venture to call himself a religious man. For what is more contrary to the artist's very nature than carelessness or neglect? What characterizes more strikingly his moral standards, what is more inherent in his very being than carefulness, than attentiveness, conscientiousness, caution, profound concern – than *care*, altogether and in general? The artist, the workman, is of course the careful human being *par excellence*; the intellectual man is that anyhow, and the artist, using his plastic gift to build a bridge between life and mind, is but a variation on the type – shall we say a peculiarly gratifying and functional freak? Yes, carefulness is the predominant trait of such a man: profound and sensitive attention to the will and the activities of the universal spirit; to change in the garment of the truth; to the just and needful thing, in other words to the will of God, whom the man of mind and spirit must serve, heedless of the hatred he arouses among stupid or frightened people, people obstinately attached by their interests to obsolete or evil phases of the age.

Well, then, the artist, the poet – by virtue of his care not only for his own product but for the Good, the True, and the will of God – he is a religious man. So be it. After all, that was what Goethe meant, when he extolled the human lot in those loving-kindly words:

> *Denkt er ewig sich ins Rechte,*
> *Ist er ewig schön und gross.*

Again, and in other words: for me and my kind the religious is lodged in the human. Not that my humanism springs from a deification of humanity – verily there is small occasion for that! Who could find the heart, contemplating this crackbrained species of ours, to indulge in optimistic rhetoric, when his words are daily given the lie by the harsh and bitter facts? Daily we see it commit all the crimes in the Decalogue; daily we despair of its future; all too well we understand why the angels in heaven from the day of its creation have turned up their noses at sight of the Creator's incomprehensible partiality for this doubtful handiwork of his. And yet I feel we must not, however well-founded our doubts, be betrayed into mere cynicism and contempt for the human race. We must not – despite all the evidence of its fantastic vileness – forget its great and honourable traits, revealed in the shape of art, science, the quest for truth, the creation of beauty, the conception of justice. Yes, it is true, we succumb to spiritual death when we show ourselves callous to that great mystery on which we are touching whenever we utter the words 'man' and 'humanity'.

Spiritual death. The words sound alarmingly religious; they sound deadly serious. For everybody, but most particularly for the artist, it is a matter of spiritual life or spiritual death; it is, to use the religious terminology, a matter of salvation. I am convinced that that writer is a lost man who betrays the things of the spirit by refusing to face and decide for himself the human problem, put, as it is to-day, in political terms. He will inevitably be stunted. And not alone will his work suffer, his talent decline, until he is incapable of giving life to anything he produces. No, even his earlier work, created before he thus rendered himself culpable, and once good and living, will cease to be so, it will crumble to dust before men's eyes. Such is my belief; I have such cases in mind.

Have I said too much, in saying that the human being is a great mystery? Whence does he come? He springs from nature, from animal nature, and behaves unmistakably after his kind. But in him nature becomes conscious of herself. She seems to have brought him forth not solely to make him lord over his own being – that is only a phrase for something with much deeper meaning. In him she lays herself open to the spiritual; she questions, admires and judges herself in him, as in a being who is at once herself and a creature of a higher order. To become conscious, that means to acquire a conscience, to know good and evil. And nature, below the human level, does not know them. She is 'innocent'. In the human being she becomes guilty – that is the 'Fall'. The human being is nature's fall from a state of innocencey; but it is not a decline, it is rather an ascent, in that a state of conscience is higher than a state of innocence. What Christians call 'original sin' is more than just a piece of priestcraft devised to keep men under the Church's thumb. It is a profound awareness in man as a spiritual being of his own natural infirmity and proneness to err, and of his rising in spirit above it. Is that disloyalty to nature? Not at all. It is a response to her own deepest desire. For it was to the end of her own spiritualization that she brought man forth.

These are ideas both Christian and humane; and we shall do well to emphasize the Christian character of the culture of our Western world. I feel the strongest antipathy for the half-educated mob that sets itself up to 'conquer Christianity'. But equally strong is my belief that the humanity of the future – that new human and universal feeling now in process of birth, drawing life from efforts and experiments of all sorts and kinds and striven after by choice and master spirits of the age – that humanity will not exhaust itself in the spirituality of the Christian faith, in the Christian dualism of soul and body, spirit and life, truth and 'the world'.

I am convinced that of all our strivings, only those are good and worth while which contribute to the birth of this new human feeling, under whose shelter and sway, after the passing of our present forlorn and leaderless stage, all humanity will live. I am convinced that my own strivings after analysis and synthesis have meaning and value only as they stand in groping, intuitive, tentative relation to this coming birth. In fact, I believe in the coming of a new, a third humanism, distinct, in complexion and fundamental temper, from its predecessors. It will not flatter mankind, looking at it through rose-coloured glasses, for it will have had experiences of which the others knew not. It will have stout-hearted knowledge of man's dark, daemonic, radically 'natural' side; united with reverence for his superbiological, spiritual worth. The new humanity will be universal – and it will have the artist's attitude: that is, it will recognize that the immense value and beauty of the human being lie precisely in that he belongs to the two kingdoms, of nature and spirit. It will realize that no romantic conflict or tragic dualism is inherent in the fact; but rather a fruitful and engaging combination of destiny and free choice. Upon that it will base a love for humanity in which its pessimism and its optimism will cancel each other out.

When I was young, I was infatuated with that pessimistic and romantic conception of the universe which set off against each other life and spirit, sensuality and redemption, and from which art derived some most compelling effects – compelling, and yet, humanly speaking, not quite legitimate, not quite genuine. In short, I was a Wagnerite. But it is very likely in consequence of riper years that my love and my attention have more and more fixed upon a far happier and saner model: the figure of Goethe, that marvellous combination of the daemonic and the urbane in him, which made him the darling of mankind. It was not lightly that I chose – for the hero of that epic which is my lifework – a man 'blest with blessing from the heavens above and from the depths beneath.'

Jacob the father pronounced this blessing upon Joseph's head. It was not a wish that he might be blest, but a statement that he was so, and a wish for his happiness. And for me, it is the most compendious possible formulation of my ideal humanity. Wherever, in the realm of mind and personality, I find that ideal manifested, as the union of darkness and light, feeling and mind, the primitive and the civilized, wisdom and the happy heart – in short as the humanized mystery we call man: there lies my profoundest allegiance, therein my heart finds its home. Let me be clear: what I mean is no subtilization of the romantic, no refinement of barbarism. It is nature clarified, it is culture; it is the human being as artist, and art as man's guide on the difficult path toward knowledge of himself.

All love of humanity is bound up with the future; and the same is true of love of art. Art is hope. . . . I do not assert that hope for the future of mankind rests upon her shoulders; rather that she is the expression of all human hope, the image and pattern of all happily balanced humanity. I like to think – yes, I feel sure – that a future is coming, wherein we shall condemn as black magic, as the brainless, irresponsible product of instinct, all art which is not controlled by the intellect. We shall condemn it in the same degree to which it is exalted in ages weak, like the one we live in, on the human side. Art, indeed, is not all sweetness and light. But neither is she altogether the dark, blind, monstrous brood of the tellurion depths. She is not just 'life.' The artist of the future will have a clearer, happier vision of his art as 'white' magic: as a winged, hermetic, moon-sib intercessor between life and spirit. For all mediation is itself spirit.

Jacques Maritain

Jacques Maritain was the leading spokesman of this century's Catholic revival, which has also numbered among its luminaries such writers as François Mauriac and Graham Greene.In polemics which are lucid in their style and graceful in their intricacy, Maritain reapplied the philosophy of St. Thomas Aquinas in a modern context, enriching contemporary theology and revealing new metaphysical dimensions in current events. As Kenneth Burke has written, the 'mere suavity of his work restores our faith in the culture of his religion.'

Works include: 'Religion and the Modern World', 'Creative Intuition in Art and Poetry', 'Approaches to God' and 'An Introduction to Philosophy'.

I was brought up as a child in 'liberal Protestantism.' Later I made the acquaintance of the different phases of lay thought. In the end the scientist and phenomenalist philosophy of my teachers at the Sorbonne made me despair of reason. For a moment I believed I might find complete certitude in the sciences, and Félix Le Dantec thought that my fiancée and I would become disciples of his biological materialism. (The best thing that I owe to my studies at that time is that they brought me into touch, at the School of Sciences, with the woman who, ever since, in all my work, has always been at my side in a perfect and blessed union.) Bergson was the first to fulfill our deep desire for metaphysical truth by giving us back the sense of the absolute.

Before being attracted to St. Thomas Aquinas, the great influences I underwent were those of Charles Péguy, Bergson, and Léon Bloy. A year after meeting Bloy, my wife and I received Catholic baptism, choosing him as our godfather.

It was after my conversion to Catholicism that I made the acquaintance of St. Thomas. After my 'passionate pilgrimage' among all the doctrines of modern philosophers, in whom I had discovered nothing but disenchantment and splendid uncertainties, I felt, as it were, an illumination of the reason. My vocation as philosopher became clear to me. *'Woe is me should I not thomistize,'* I wrote in one of my first books. And through thirty years of work and combat I have followed in this path, with a feeling that I could understand more completely the gropings, the discoveries, and the travail of modern thought, as I tried to throw upon them more of the light which comes to us from a wisdom which, resisting the fluctuations of time, has been worked out through the centuries.

In order to advance along this way, we are constantly obliged to bring together singularly distant extremes (for no solution of our problems can be found *ready-made* in the legacy of the ancients). We are also obliged to make the difficult separation between the pure substance of those truths, which many 'moderns' reject as a mere jumble of the opinions of the past, and all the dross of prejudice, worn-out expressions, and arbitrary constructions, which many 'traditionalists' confuse with that which really deserves intellectual veneration.

I have mentioned the different phases through which I passed because they gave me the opportunity of experiencing personally the state of mind of the idealistic freethinker, of the inexperienced convert, and of the Christian who becomes aware, as his faith takes root, of the purifications to which it must be subjected. I was likewise enabled to acquire some experimental idea of what the anti-religious camp and the so-called *orthodox (bien pensant)* camp are worth. Neither of them is worth much. To my way of thinking, God trains us, through our disillusionments and mistakes, to understand at last that we must believe only in Him and not in men, which places us in the proper position to marvel at all the good which is in men in spite of everything and all the good which they do in spite of themselves.

This is not the proper place to expound propositions of speculative philosophy. I shall say only that I consider Thomistic philosophy as a living and up-to-date philosophy, having all the greater power for the conquest of new fields of discovery as its principles are firmer and more organically cemented. When they behold the succession of scientific hypotheses, certain minds are surprised that it should, to-day, be possible to draw inspiration from metaphysical principles recognized by Aristotle and Thomas Aquinas and rooted in the most ancient intellectual heritage of our kind. To this I reply that the telephone and the radio do not prevent men from still having two arms, two legs, and two lungs, from falling in love and searching for happiness like their far-away ancestors. Moreover, truth recognizes no chronological criteria and the art of the philosopher cannot be confused with that of fashion.

Going still further, it must be explained that progress takes place in the sciences of phenomena, in which the 'problem' aspect is very marked, principally by the *substitution* of one theory for another theory which took account of a lesser number of known facts and phenomena; whereas with metaphysics and philosophy, where the 'mystery' aspect predominates, progress takes place principally by *deeper penetration*. In addition, the different philosophical systems, however ill-founded they may be, constitute, when taken together, a kind of virtual and fluent philosophy, overlapping contrary formulations and hostile doctrines and supported by the elements of truth they all contain. If, therefore, a body of doctrine exists among men, entirely supported by true principles, it will progressively (and more or less tardily, due to the laziness of its advocates) incorporate in itself and *realize* this virtual philosophy, thereby giving it form and organization. Such is my idea of 'progress' in philosophy.

If after that I say that the metaphysics which I hold to be well founded in truth can be described as critical realism and as a philosophy of intelligence and of being, or still more precisely of *existing* considered as the act and perfection of all perfections, these formulas will doubtless be of interest only to specialists. A few reflections on the historical significance of modern philosophy will no doubt be more appropriate.

In the Middle Ages philosophy was, in fact, usually treated as an instrument in the service of theology. Culturally, it was not in the state required by its nature. The coming of a philosophical or profane wisdom which had completed its own formation for itself and according to its own finalities, responded, therefore, to a historical necessity. But unfortunately this work was brought about under the emblem of separatism and a sectarian rationalism; Descartes *separated* philosophy from all higher wisdom, from everything in man which comes from above man. I am certain that what the world and civilization have lacked for three centuries has been a philosophy which would have developed its autonomous exigencies in a Christian climate, a wisdom of reason not closed but open to the wisdom of grace. Reason must battle to-day with an irrationalist deification of elemental and instinctive forces, which threatens to ruin the whole of civilization. In this struggle, reason's task is one of integration; understanding that the intelligence is not the enemy of mystery but rather lives by it, it must *re-enter into intelligence* with the irrational world of affectivity and instinct, as with the world of the will, of liberty and of love, as with the supra-rational world of grace and the Divine Life.

The dynamic harmony of the degrees of knowledge will be made manifest at the same time. From this standpoint, the problem peculiar to the age we are entering will be, so it seems, to reconcile *science* and *wisdom*. The sciences themselves seem to invite the intelligence to this task. We see them being stripped of the traces of materialistic and mechanistic metaphysics which hid their true features. They call for a philosophy of nature, and from the marvellous progress of contemporary physics, the savant can regain a sense of the mystery announced by the atom, as by the universe. A critique of knowledge formed in a truly realist and metaphysical spirit thenceforth has a chance to be heard when it predicates the existence of structures of knowledge specifically and hierarchically distinct (distinct, but not separate) and shows that they correspond to original types of explanation which could not be substituted one for the other.

The Greeks recognized the great truth that contemplation is in itself superior to action. But they at once transformed it into a great error: they believed that humankind exists for the benefit of a few intellectuals. According to their way of thinking, philosophers were a category of specialists living a superhuman life, and ordinary human life, which is civic or political life, existed for their service. For the service of the latter, in turn, there was the subhuman life of labour, that is to say, ultimately, the life of the slave. The lofty truth of the superiority of the contemplative life was thus tied to a contempt for labour and to the evil of slavery.

All this was transfigured by Christianity. Christianity taught men that love is worth more than intelligence. It transformed the notion of contemplation which henceforth did not stop with the intellect but with the love of God, its objects. It restored to action its human significance of service to one's neighbour and rehabilitated labour by showing forth in it, as it were, an import of natural redemption and a natural prefiguration of the communication of charity. It summoned to the contemplation of saints and to perfection, not a few specialists or privileged persons, but all men, who, symmetrically, are all bound by the law of labour. Man is *at once* Homo faber and Homo sapiens, but he is Homo faber before becoming truly in act, and in order to become, Homo sapiens. Thus the Greek idea of the superiority of the contemplative life was preserved by Christianity, but through a transformation and by freeing it from the error by which it had been tainted.

The contemplation of saints completes and consummates a natural aspiration to contemplation which is consubstantial in man and of which the wise men of India and Greece in particular give testimony. In supernatural contemplation, it is through love that the knowledge of divine things becomes experimental and fruitful. For the very reason that it is the work of love in act, it passes also into action by virtue of the very generosity and abundance of love, which is the gift of self. It is then that action issues forth from the superabundance of contemplation, and this is why, far from suppressing action or obstructing it, contemplation gives it life. It is in this sense, which goes back to the essential generosity of the contemplation of love, that with Bergson we must recognize in the superabundance and excess of the gift of self shown by the Christian mystics, a sign of their success in reaching the heroic peaks of human life.

The pursuit of supreme contemplation and the pursuit of supreme liberty are two aspects of the same pursuit. In the order of the spiritual life, man aspires to perfect and absolute freedom, and therefore to a superhuman state. The men of wisdom of all times have given evidence of this. The function of the law is a function of protection and education of liberty, the function of a pedagogue. At the conclusion of this tutelage, the perfect man is freed from every servitude, even, St. Paul says, from the servitude of the law, because he does spontaneously what the law demands and is one spirit with the Creator.

The pursuit of liberty is still, to my way of thinking, at the bottom of the social and political problem. But here, in the order of temporal life, it is not a divine liberty which is the object of our desires, but rather a liberty proportionate to the state of man and to the natural possibilities of our earthly existence. We must make no mistake about the nature of the object thus pursued. It is not simply the protection of *free will* in each of us, nor is it the *liberty of expansion* of the human persons which make up a people and participate in its virtues. Organized society is intended to develop conditions of life in common which, while insuring first of all advantages and peace to the whole, help each person in a positive manner progressively to conquer this freedom of expansion which consists above all in the flowering of oral and rational life.

So justice and love are the very foundations of the life of society, which must subject to truly human advantages all manner of material advantages, technical progress, and the implements of power, which also form part of society's common good.

I believe that historical conditions and the yet inferior state of development of humanity make it difficult for organized society fully to reach its objective, and that in respect to the possibilities which the Gospel brings us and the demands it makes on us in the social-temporal domain, we are still in a prehistoric age. As we have seen in the psychoses of the masses adoring Stalin or Hitler, or dreaming of exterminating certain classes which they consider diabolical, such as 'the Reds' or the 'Fascists' or 'the Jews,' human collectivities bear such a burden of animality, easily inclined to morbidity, that it will take centuries still for the human personality to be able really to take on among the masses the breadth of life to which it aspires. We can see, then, that the objective toward which organized society tends by its very nature is to procure the common advantage of the multitude in such a manner that the individual person, not only the one belonging to a privileged class but the members of the whole mass, may truly reach that measure of independence which is proper to civilized life and which is insured alike by the economic guarantees of work and property, political rights, civic virtues, and the cultivation of the mind.

These concepts belong to wider general views which seem to me most fittingly designated under the term *integral humanism*, and which involve a whole philosophy of modern history. Such a humanism, considering man in the integrality of his natural and his supernatural being and setting no limits *a priori* on the descent of divinity into man, can also be called Humanism of the Incarnation.

In the social-temporal order, it does not call on man to sacrifice himself for any imperialism, be it of the race, of the class, or of the nation. It calls upon him to sacrifice himself to a better life for his brothers and to the concrete good of the community of human persons. Thus it can only be a heroic humanism.

It has often been remarked that middle-class liberalism, which tries to base everything on the individual considered as a little god and on his gracious pleasure, on absolute freedom of property, commerce, and the pleasures of life, must inevitably lead to a despotic paternalism of the state. The reign of the Greater Number produces an omnipotent state of the ruminant or plutocratic type. Communism may be regarded as a reaction against this individualism. It claims to lead to the absolute release of man who is supposed to become the god of history, but in reality this release, presuming that it were accomplished, would then be that of man taken collectively, not of the human person. Society as an economic community would enslave the whole life of the person, because economic functions would become the essential work of civil society instead of serving the liberty of expansion of the person. We already see in Russia that what is represented as the release of man taken collectively would be the enslavement of all individuals.

As for the anti-communist and anti-individualist reactions of the totalitarian or dictatorial type, it is not in the name of the social community and of the liberty of man considered collectively, but in the name of the sovereign dignity of the state, which is a state of the carnivorous type, or in the name of the spirit of a people, or in the name of a race and blood, that they would turn man over bodily to a social entity in which the person of the chief is the only one to enjoy, properly speaking, the privileges of a human personality. This is why totalitarian states, having need for themselves of the entire devotion of the human person for which they have neither feeling nor respect, inevitably seek to find a principle of human exaltation in myths of external grandeur and in the never-ending struggle for power and prestige. By its very nature this leads to war and the auto-destruction of the civilized community. If there are churchmen who count on dictatorships of this kind to promote the religion of Christ and Christian civilization, they forget that the totalitarian phenomenon is an aberrant religious phenomenon in which a kind of earthly mysticism devours every other sort of mysticism and will tolerate no other one beside itself.

Confronted with bourgeois liberalism, communism, and totalitarianism, what we need is a new solution, at once personalistic and communal, which views human society as the organization of liberties. We are thus led to a conception of democracy differing fundamentally from that of Jean-Jacques Rousseau and which we might call *pluralist*, because it requires that the state insure the organic liberties of the different spiritual families and the different social bodies assembled within it, beginning with the natural basic community, the society of the family. The tragedy of modern democracies is that, under the appearances of an error – the deification of a fictitious individual closed to all realities from above – they have sought something good, the expansion of the personality open to realities from above and to the common service of justice and friendship. Our personalist democracy is really inconceivable without those super-elevations which nature and temporal civilizations receive, in their own order, from the energies of the Christian leaven.

I am certain that the coming of such a democracy, which presupposes class antagonism overcome, requires that we go beyond capitalism and beyond socialism, which are both tainted by a materialistic conception of life.

I would remark that Christians to-day find themselves confronted, in the social-temporal order, with problems similar to those which their forefathers encountered, in the sphere of the philosophy of nature, in the sixteenth and seventeenth centuries. At that time modern physics and astronomy, which were beginning, were bound up with the philosophical systems set up against tradition. The champions of tradition did not know how to make the necessary distinctions. They took sides against what was going to become modern science at the same time as against the philosophical errors which, in the beginning, parasitized it. Three centuries have been necessary to clear up this misunderstanding, if it can be said that the world is indeed clear of it. It would be disastrous to-day to revive the same errors in the sphere of practical and social philosophy.

Pope Pius XI said that the great scandal of the nineteenth century was the divorce between the working classes and the Church. In the temporal order, the moral secession of the working masses with regard to the political community is a tragedy of a like nature. The awakening of what the socialist vocabulary calls class consciousness in the working multitudes appears to us as an important step forward if we regard it as the arousing of a consciousness of a vocation. But it has been tied up to an historic calamity in that this awakening of consciousness has been poisoned by the evangel of despair and social welfare which is at the bottom of the Marxian idea of class strife and the dictatorship of the proletariat. In the nineteenth century, the blindness of the owning classes thrust the working masses into just this *secessionist* concept which Marx advocated and which calls upon the proletarians of all countries to consider no other common good than that of their own class.

Whoever has pondered these fundamental facts and the history of the labour movement, has understood that the temporal and spiritual problem of the *reintegration of the masses* is the central problem of our times. It was only an artificial and illusory solution of this problem to endeavour, as in National-Socialist Germany, to manufacture a race of happy slaves through violence, accompanied by certain material improvements which are good in themselves but which are brought about in a spirit of domination, and by a psychotechnic solicitude which is bound to satisfy appetites by putting them to sleep. However difficult, slow, and painful it may be, the reintegration of the proletariat in the national community, to collaborate heart and soul in the work of the community and not to exercise a class dictatorship over it, can take place *really*, that is to say *humanly*, only by a remoulding of the social structures accomplished in a spirit of justice. I am not sufficiently naïve to believe that this reintegration can be brought about without collisions and without sacrifices, on the one hand for the well-being of favoured sons of fortune and on the other for the theories and the destructive instincts of revolutionary fanatics. But I am certain that it requires, above all, a free co-operation on the part of the *élite* of the working class and the masses who follow their lead, in a better general understanding of historical realities, and a consciousness of the dignity of the human being as worker and citizen, which is not effaced but rather heightened. In the same way, the return of the masses to Christianity will be brought about only through love – and I mean that love which is stronger than death, the fire of the Gospel.

We shall never give up the hope of a new Christendom, of a new temporal order inspired by Christianity. Now, if it is true that the means must correspond to the end and are themselves the end, as it were in the state of formation and preparation, it is then clear that in order to prepare a Christian social order, Christian means are needed; that is to say, true means, just means, means which are animated, even when they are perforce harsh, by a true spirit of love.

Nothing can be graver or more scandalous than to see, as we have seen for some years past in certain countries, the iniquitous and barbarous means employed by men who invoke a Christian order and a Christian civilization. Aldous Huxley, among others, denounced the madness of wishing to produce good ends by bad means. Henri de Man explained that in the means the end is already performed. Will Christians ever understand? It is a truth laid down in the very nature of things that Christendom will be made over by Christian means or will be completely unmade.

Pessimism is always the victim of its own deceit. It disregards the great law which might be called the law of the double energy movement of history. While the wear and tear of time naturally dissipates and degrades the things of this world and the energy of history, the creative forces which are characteristic of the spirit and of liberty, and are also their witness, and which normally find their point of application in the effort of the few – destined thereby to sacrifice – constantly revitalize the quality of this energy. Such is the work accomplished in history by the sons of God; such is the work of Christians if they do not give the lie to their name.

This work is not understood at all if it is imagined that it claims to be able to set up a state in the world from which all evil and all injustice would be banished. Naturally, on this ground it would be too easy, in view of the results obtained, stupidly to dismiss Christians as Utopians. What the Christian has to do is to maintain and increase in the world an internal tension and that movement of slow and painful delivery, which comes from the invisible powers of truth and justice, goodness and love, acting upon the mass in opposition to them. This work cannot be in vain and it cannot but bear fruit.

Woe to the world should the Christians turn their back on it, should they fail to do *their job*, which is to heighten here on earth the charge and tension of spirituality; should they listen to those blind leaders of the blind who seek the means to order and do good in things which are in their very nature dissolution and death. We have no illusions about the misery of human nature and the wickedness of the world. But we have no illusions either about the blindness and the harm worked by those pseudo-realists who cultivate and exalt evil to fight against evil and who look upon the Gospel as a decorative myth which could not be taken seriously without wrecking the machinery of the world. They themselves do their part in ruining this unhappy world and driving it to folly and despair.

One of the gravest lessons we receive from the experience of life is that, in the practical behaviour of most of us, all those things which are in themselves good - science, technical progress, culture, etc., the knowledge of moral laws too, and even religious faith itself, faith in the living God, all these things, *without love and good will*, only serve, in fact, to make men more wicked and more unhappy. This is because, without love and charity, man turns into evil the best that is in him.

Once we have understood this, we no longer put our hope here on earth save in that good will of which the Gospel speaks, in that obscure strength of a bit of real goodness which brings forth life and brings it forth without cease in the most hidden recesses of things. Nothing is more destitute, nothing is more secret, nothing is nearer to the weakness of childhood. And there is no more fundamental, no more effective wisdom than that simple and tenacious confidence – not in the weapons of force and cleverness and malice, which though they always triumph at the outset, a grain of sand suffices to ruin, but in the resources of personal courage and good will. Through this kind of lightness of heart flows the force of nature and of the Author of nature.

Malcolm Muggeridge

Malcolm Muggeridge once reported with approval the saying 'only dead fish swim with the stream'; he has spent his long working life swimming against the current of fashionable ideas. Placing day to day events in their widest moral and spiritual contexts, he is a journalist in the grand tradition of Doctor Johnson and William Cobbett. By his remarkable honesty about his inner travails he has made his life a sort of symbol of his generation's quest for belief.

Works include: 'Something Beautiful for God', 'Jesus Rediscovered', 'The Green Stick' and 'The Infernal Grove'.

In trying to formulate what I believe I have to begin with what I disbelieve. I disbelieve in progress, the pursuit of happiness, and all the concomitant notions and projects for creating a society in which human beings find ever greater contentment by being given in ever greater abundance the means to satisfy their material and bodily hopes and desires. In other words, I consider that the way of life in urbanized, rich countries as it exists today, and as it it likely to go on developing, is probably the most degraded and unillumined ever to come to pass on earth. The time in which I have been consciously alive seems to me to have been quite exceptionally destructive, murderous and brutal. More people have been killed and terrorized, more driven from their homes and native places; more of the past's heritage has been destroyed, more lies propagated and base persuasion engaged in, with less compensatory achievement in art, literature and imaginative understanding, than in any comparable period of history.

Ever since I can remember, the image of earthly power, whether in the guise of schoolmaster, mayor, judge, prime minister, monarch, or any other, has seemed to me derisory. I was enchanted when I first read in the *Pensées* (Pascal being one of the small, sublime band of fellow-humans to whom one may turn and say in the deepest humility: 'I agree') about how magistrates and rulers had to be garbed in their ridiculous ceremonial robes, crowns and diadems. Otherwise, who would not see through their threadbare pretensions? I am conscious of having been ruled by buffoons, taught by idiots, preached at by hypocrites, and preyed upon by charlatans in the guise of advertisers and other professional persuaders, as well as verbose demagogues and ideologues of many opinions, all false.

Nor, as far as I am concerned, is there any recompense in the so-called achievements of science. It is true that in my lifetime more progress has been made in unravelling the composition and mechanism of the material universe than previously in the whole of recorded time. This does not at all excite my mind, or even my curiosity. The atom has been split; the universe has been discovered, and will soon be explored. Neither achievement has any bearing on what alone interests me – which is why life exists, and what is the significance, if any, of my minute and so transitory part in it. All the world in a grain of sand; all the universe, too. If I could understand a grain of sand I should understand everything. Why, then, should going to the Moon and Mars, or spending a holiday along the Milky Way, be expected to advance me further in my quest than going to Manchester and Liverpool, or spending a holiday in Brighton?

Education, the great mumbo-jumbo and fraud of the age, purports to equip us to live, and is prescribed as a universal remedy for everything from juvenile deliquency to premature senility. For the most part, it only serves to enlarge stupidity, inflate conceit, enhance credulity, and put those subjected to it at the mercy of brainwashers with printing presses, radio and television at their disposal. I have seen pictures of huge, ungainly prehistoric monsters who developed such a weight of protective shell that they sank under its burden and became extinct. Our civilization likewise is sinking under the burden of nuclear defence, and may well soon be extinct. As this fact sinks into the collective consciousness, the resort to drugs, dreams, fantasies, and other escapist devices, particularly sex, becomes ever more marked.

Living thus in the twilight of a spent civilization, amidst its ludicrous and frightening shadows, what is there to believe? Curiously enough, these twilit circumstances provide a setting in which, as it seems to me, the purpose which lies behind them stands out with particular clarity. As human love only shines in all its splendour when the last tiny glimmer of desire has been extinguished, so we have to make the world a wilderness to find God. The meaning of the universe lies beyond history as love lies beyond desire. That meaning shines forth in moments of illumination (which come and go so unaccountably; though, I am thankful to say, never quite ceasing – a sound as of music, far, far away, and drowned by other more tumultuous noises, but still to be faintly and fitfully heard) with an inconceivable clarity and luminosity. It breaks like a crystalline dawn out of darkness, and the deeper the darkness the more crystalline the dawn.

Let me express it, as I have often thought of it, in terms of a stage. In the middle is the workaday world where we live our daily lives, earning a living, reading newspapers, exchanging money, recording votes, chattering and eating and desiring. I call this the Café Limbo. On the left of the stage is an area of darkness within which shapes and movements can be faintly discerned, and inconclusive noises heard; sounds and sweet airs which, as on Caliban's Island, give delight and hurt not. I call this Life. The right of the stage is bright with arc-lamps like a television studio. This is where history is unfolded and news is made; this is where we live our public, collective lives, seat and unseat rulers, declare wars and negotiate peace, glow with patriotism and get carried away with revolutionary zeal, enact laws, declaim rhetoric, swear eternal passion and sink into abysses of desolation. I call this Legend.

Across this triple stage, between Life, the Café Limbo and the Legend, a drama is endlessly presented. Two forces shape the play – the Imagination which belongs to Life, and the Will which belongs to the Legend. Out of the Imagination comes love, understanding, goodness, self-abnegation; every true synthesis ever grasped or to be grasped. Out of the Will comes lust, hatred, cupidity, adulation, power, oratory; every false antithesis ever propounded or to be propounded. Those who belong exclusively or predominantely to Life are saints, mystics and artists. In extreme cases – Christ, for instance – they have to be killed. (This is superbly explained in the famous Grand Inquisitor passage in *The Brothers Karamazov*, Dostoevsky being, like Pascal, of the small band.) Those who belong exclusively or predominantly to the Legend are power-maniacs, rulers, heroes, demagogues and liberators. In extreme cases – Hitler, for instance – they bring about their own destruction. In Life there is suffering, deprivation and sanity; in the Legend, happiness, abundance and madness.

Most of us spend the greater part of our time in the Café Limbo, casting an occasional glance in the direction of Life, and more than an occasional one in the direction of the Legend. Laughter is our best recourse, with the bar to provide a fillip as and when required. The Café Limbo is licensed. When a character passes from the Legend into Life he brings some of the light with him; shining like a glow-worm, until gradually the light subsides and goes out, swallowed up in the darkness of Life.

The same pattern may be traced more particularly and tragically in a single countenance, as anyone will be aware who has had occasion to watch over a loved face hovering between sanity and madness. (And many have. For as we abolish the ills and pains of the flesh we multiply those of the mind, so that by the time mankind are finally delivered from disease and decay – all pasteurized, their genes counted and rearranged, fitted with new replaceable plastic organs, able to eat, fornicate, and perform other physical functions innocuously and hygienically as and when desired – they will all be mad, and the world one huge psychiatric ward.) You study the loved, distracted face as a scholar might study some ancient manuscript, looking for a key to its incomprehensibility. What you see is a fight to the death between the Will and the Imagination. If the former wins, then the flickering light will be put out for ever; if the latter, it will shine again, to burn with a steady radiance. Oh, beloved, you have come back to me.

I am well aware that, psychiatrically speaking, this is nonsensical. Yet I believe it. I see the two forces struggling for mastery in each individual soul; in mine, in all men's: in each collectivity, throughout our earth and throughout the vast universe. One is of darkness and one of light; one wants to drag us down into the dark trough to rut and gorge there, and the other to raise us up into the azure sky, beyond appetite, where love is all-embracing, all-encompassing, and the dark confusion of life sorts itself out, like an orderly, smiling countryside suddenly glimpsed from a high hill. One is the Devil and the other God. I have known both, and I believe in both.

For we Western Europeans the Christian religion has expressed this ancient, and, as I consider, obvious dichotomy in terms of breathtaking simplicity and sublimity. It was not the first word on the subject, nor will it be the last; but it is still our Word. I accept it. I believe, as is written in the New Testament, that if we would save our lives we must lose them; that we cannot live by bread alone; that we must die in the flesh to be reborn in the spirit, and that the flesh lusts contrary to the spirit and the spirit contrary to the flesh; that God cannot see a sparrow fall to the ground without concern, and has counted the hairs of each head, so that all that lives deserves our respect and reverence, and no one man can conceivably be more important, of greater significance, or in any way more deserving of consideration than any other.

It is true that these basic propositions of Christianity have got cluttered up with dogma of various kinds which I find often incomprehensible, irrelevant and even repugnant. All the same I should be proud and happy to be able to call myself a Christian; to dare to measure myself against that immeasurably high standard of human values and human behaviour. In this I take comfort from another saying of Pascal, thrown out like a lifeline to all sceptical minds throughout the ages – that whosoever looks for God has found Him.

At its most obscurantist and debased, the Christian position still seems to me preferable to any scientific-materialist one, however cogent and enlightened. The evangelist with his lurid tract calling upon me to repent for the Day of Judgement is at hand, is a burning and shining light compared with the eugenist who claims the right to decide in his broiler-house mind which lives should be protracted and which must be put out; or with the colporteurs of sterility who so complacently and self-righteously display their assortment of contraceptives to the so-called backward peoples of the world as our civilization's noblest achievement and most precious gift.

The absurdities of the Kingdom of Heaven, as conceived in the minds of simple believers, are obvious enough – pearly gates, angelic choirs, golden crowns and shining raiment. But what are we to think of the (in Johnson's excellent phrase) sheer unresisting imbecility of the Kingdom of Heaven on Earth, as envisaged and recommended by the most authoritative and powerful voices of our time? The Gross National Product rising for evermore, and its beneficiaries, rich in hire-purchase, stupefied with the telly and with sex, comprehensively educated, told by Professor Hoyle how the world began and by Canon Collins how it will end; on the broad highways venturing forth, three lanes a side, with lay-bys to rest in and birth pills to keep them *intacta*, if not *virgo*, as an extra thrill blood spattering the tarmac; heaven lying about them in the supermarket, the rainbow ending in the nearest bingo hall, leisure burgeoning out in multitudinous shining aerials rising like dreaming spires into the sky; happiness in as many colours as there are pills – green and yellow and blue and red and shining white; many mansions, mansions of light and chromium, climbing ever upwards. This Kingdom, surely, can only be for posterity an unending source of wry derision – always assuming there is to be any posterity. The backdrop, after all, is the mushroom cloud; as the Gadarene herd frisk and frolic they draw ever nearer to the cliff's edge.

I recognize, of course, that this statement of belief is partly governed by the circumstance that I am old, and in at most a decade or so will be dead. In earlier years I should doubtless have expressed things differently. Now, the prospect of death overshadows all others. I am like a man on a sea voyage nearing his destination. When I embarked I worried about having a cabin with a porthole, whether I should be asked to sit at the captain's table, who were the more attractive and important passengers. All such considerations become pointless when I shall soon be disembarking.

As I do not believe that earthly life can bring any lasting satisfaction, the prospect of death holds no terrors. Those saints who pronounced themselves in love with death displayed, I consider, the best of sense; not a Freudian death-wish. Likewise Pastor Bonhoeffer when he told his Nazi guards, as they took him away to be executed, that for them it was an end but for him a beginning; in that place of darkest evil he, the victim, shining and radiant. The world that I shall soon be leaving seems more than ever beautiful; especially its remoter parts, grass and trees and sea and rivers and little streams and sloping hills, where the image of eternity is more clearly stamped than among streets and houses. Those I love I can love even more, since I have nothing to ask of them but their love; the passion to accumulate possessions, or to be noticed and important, is too evidently absurd to be any longer entertained.

A sense of how extraordinarily happy I have been, and of enormous gratitude to my creator, overwhelms me often. I believe with a passionate, unshakeable conviction that in all circumstances and at all times life is a blessed gift; that the spirit which animates it is one of love, not hate or indifference, of light, not darkness, of creativity, not destruction, of order, not chaos; that, since all life, men, creatures, plants, as well as insensate matter, and all that is known about it, now and henceforth, has been benevolently, not malevolently, conceived, when the eyes see no more and the mind thinks no more, and this hand now writing is inert, whatever lies beyond will similarly be benevolently, not malevolently conceived. If it is nothing, then for nothingness I offer thanks; if another mode of existence, with this old worn-out husk of a body left behind, like a butterfly extricating itself from its chrysalis, and this floundering, muddled mind, now at best seeing through a glass darkly, given a longer range and a new precision, then for that likewise I offer thanks.

W. V. Quine

The pre-eminent philosopher of our time, W. V. Quine pushes forward the frontiers of scepticism. His colourful and witty treatises on logic persistently and successfully attack assumptions made by sceptics before him. His various innovations are now emerging as a coherent and systematic world-view comparable to Wittgenstein's in the magnitude of its intellectual achievement.

Works include: 'Methods of Logic', 'From a Logical Point of View', 'The Ways of Paradox' and 'Word and Object'.

The world is a multitude of minute twitches in the void. They are microphysical events, related one to another by any of three or four forces. It is convenient to say that what do the twitching are particles, but the stricter line is to rest with the twitches and let the particles go. A particle is subject to identity crises; it can pass so close to another, for instance, that it makes no sense to say, from there on, which was which. The particle may be regarded as just a conceptually convenient serial grouping of microphysical events, in much the way that a crowd or a race is a conceptually convenient grouping of persons. Like a crowd or a race, it need not be assured of precise identification at all points. Still it enjoys a more stubborn integrity that the crowd or the race, and this makes the particle concept so convenient as to be practically indispensable.

In declaring for microphysical events, or indeed particles, I am not denying the robust reality of our ordinary objects, our sticks and stones. Just as a forest is seen from afar as a mass in which no tree stands forth, so the stick or stone is seen as a mass in which no particle stands forth, but the stick or stone, like the forest, is none the less real for that. Eyesight sharper than ours could show these familiar solids to be swarms of vibrating molecules. Discrimination of still smaller particles does ultimately exceed all optical possibilities, because of the coarseness of light itself; but physicists have their more devious resources.

How something looks is a relation of the object to the eye of the beholder. An ink blot is continuous to the naked eye and diffuse when magnified. We can imagine extra-terrestrials who are sensitive to radiation outside our visual range, and they might see vaporous clouds, unimaginably coloured, where we see only emptiness. But everything in the world comes down to elementary particles or microphysical events, whatever the point of view.

Everything in the world. The qualification is significant, for it sets aside the question of abstract objects such as properties and numbers.

These are not in the world, for they are not anywhere; but it may still be held that there *are* such objects, out of space, out of time. We should be happy to repudiate them, but wishful thinking is not the way of science or true philosophy. Numbers, surely, are appealed to in theoretical physics at every turn. I am not thinking of the mere uses of specific numerals; words used need not always be presumed to name anything. The point is rather that numbers are invoked collectively, not just by name but as values of variables. On any reasonable criterion for assessing the ontological commitments of a theory, our natural science is as firmly committed to numbers as it is to anything. Accepting science as I do, subject of course to subsequent scientific correction, I am constrained to acknowledge the reality of numbers.

The same applies to functions, and to classes. Actually, we know from set theory that the classes are enough; they can serve also as numbers and functions. But I draw the line at other abstract objects, notably properties. These are beset with problems of identity and other logical difficulties, and anyway they serve no really clear purposes that are not served by classes.

I said that everything in the world resolves into elementary particles or microphysical events, and then I noted that this does not apply to abstract objects. It applies emphatically to man, however, and to the mind of man. Mind is part of the activity of a physical object, the human animal. Self-awareness is just one of the various perspectives upon a physical object. Here the object is oneself, observed from within.

> *Some pow'r did us the giftie grant*
> *To see oursels as others can't.*

One's acts and decisions are activities of a physical object, and are subject to outside causes as are the movements of any physical objects. If nature is deterministic, so that its state at any time is causally determined by its previous states, then determinism applies in particular to human behaviour. This point has been resisted by some philosophers, who see it as precluding freedom of the will.

It must be said that determinism has also been challenged from a very different quarter. The quantum physics of microphysical events has engendered quandaries regarding the very notion of cause and effect as traditionally conceived. However, that is an unlikely quarter in which to seek loopholes for freedom of the will.

I hold rather, as have many before me, that determinism has no bearing on freedom of the will. One's behaviour is free when it is caused by one's internal drives, be they ideals or appetites; and it is no curb to freedom that these drives are caused in turn.

Given then that one's acts are determined ultimately by outside causes, is there any warrant for praise or blame? There is indeed. Good men, like good paintings and good machines, are justly admired and commended, and bad ones disparaged; and there need be no suspension of causality. On the contrary, praise and reward help to cause good behaviour as well as good art and good technology; and censure and punishment can help to discourage the bad.

Praise and blame in the moral sphere raise the problem, still, of how our standards of good and evil are justified. The hypothesis of the existence of God has offered an objective basis for moral values, in God's decrees. Is this hypothesis not comparable to scientific hypotheses, which are supported by the explanations that they offer of known states of affairs? It is not. What this hypothesis explains is not a known state of affairs, but only a desired one: the objectivity of moral values. The God hypothesis is, insofar a case of wishful thinking, equal and opposite to the case noted earlier of the wishful repudiation of numbers and kindred abstract objects.

Theism is rich in comforts. It is associated with the dream of life after death and of reward for virtue unrewarded on earth. On the latter point, and the correlative threat of hellfire, religion has been a boon to society, promoting charity and curbing crime. These social benefits, unlike mere wishful thinking, are a sound reason for propounding religious doctrine. Whether they are a sufficient reason, I hesitate to say; but they afford no evidence of truth.

Arguments for the truth of theism there have indeed been, but they fall short. The intricacies of organic nature have been said to bear witness to God as designer; but then God's *modus operandi* is fully as hard to explain as the intricacies of organic nature. Another argument begins by defining God as a being that necessarily exists. I am spared trying to do justice to this elusive argument, for it is swept aside if we reject as gratuitous, as I do, the very notion of metaphysical necessity. Necessity makes sense to me only relative to passing contexts: something holds necessarily, relative to a going dialogue, if it follows from the beliefs or assumptions shared by the participants of the dialogue at the time. Absolutely there are just the true and the false, without benefit of adverb.

Metaphysical necessity is one of the mainstays of theology that hark back to Aristotle. Another of them is a startling restriction on contingent statements about the future: that they are now neither true nor false, and become true only when the event is clinched. The theological bearing of the doctrine is as follows. If the sentences were true all along, then God in his omniscience would already know they were true, and thus the future would be determined in advance by God's knowledge; and determinism is thought, however wrongly, to preclude free will. In my philosophy this hedging of futures gets short shrift, as did metaphysical necessity. I view statements about the future as true or false and forever, though in most cases we shall never know which; and determinism is as may be.

Notions and distinctions have been devised with a view to theism, we see, that are better cleared away. But, we may still ask, do we know that theism is false? 'Know' is a pernicious verb. Science is refined common sense, and is fallible at various points in various degrees. It is open always to correction by further scientific advances, but there are no alternative avenues of discovery. Barring one or another inordinate reinterpretation of terms, it can be affirmed with all the confidence of sound scientific judgment that there is no God or afterlife.

What then is the ground of moral values? Utterly human. Partly they are imposed by legislation, child-rearing, and religion, and partly they are presumably inherited through natural selection. Their point, broadly, is the fostering of society by reconciling the conflicting desires of its members. Moral issues can arise, therefore, over the relative weighting of benefits. One moralist may espouse charity for the retarded; another may interpose reservations on eugenic grounds. One may oppose torture categorically; another may condone it for punishment or for extorting information beneficial to society. One who favours torture for its own sake, however, represents no moral position, and indeed conflict usually reflects rather an aloofness from moral values than disagreement over them.

Directed as it is to the welfare of a society, morality hinges on demarcation of the pertinent society. An isolated tribe could rest with a crystalline moral law, seemingly absolute and eternal, recognized by all and obeyed by most. Conflict between societies is outside of society and is thus morally neutral, until we widen our horizons and fuse many societies as one. For most of us the demarcation of society is manifold, marking tighter societies that variously overlap within looser ones; thus family, clan, nation, culture, species, phylum, posterity. Besides the moral issues over the weighting of benefits, therefore, there arise moral issues over the weighting of beneficiaries. Moral dilemma is rife.

I might gracefully conclude this brief sheaf of beliefs with some cheerful ones about the future of man. My practice down the years of withstanding the lures of wishful thinking has steeled me, but I will say what I can.

Man's abuse of the earth's atmosphere, hydrosphere, chthonosphere, and biosphere has aroused at last a laudable host of nature lovers and conservationists, for whose success my hopes are only moderately high but immoderately fervent. The appalling population explosion has become the concern of increasingly vigorous campaigns worldwide for family planning, and I gather that in recent statistics there is some cheer for sanguine hearts. The soaring of violence in recent decades threatens to trim the figures in harsher ways. Meanwhile man's understanding of the cosmos and its fine texture has advanced at an unprecedented rate and is accelerating. Young people athirst for knowledge have prospects of unimaginable gratification, if the fabric holds.

Bertrand Russell

*N*o *contemporary philosopher has captured the imagination of the English-speaking world to the same degree as Bertrand Russell. He revived the British tradition of Berkely and Hume, returning philosophy to something more exacting than it had become in the intervening period. In his philosophy of Logical Atomism he reduced the complexity of human experience to one version of its simplest elements, and so made himself the father of modern logic. Going on to reconstruct the world from its simplest elements, he applied his incisive methodology to many different areas of human knowledge, including religion, ethics, sociology, educational theory and politics. In all fields of thought he showed a vigorous concern for the freedom and happiness of the individual although much of what he wrote caused outrage. He himself said 'The point of philosophy is to start with something so simple as not to seem worth stating and to end with something so paradoxical that no-one will believe it.'*

Works include: 'Principia Mathematica', 'The Problems of Philosophy', 'The Conquest of Happiness' and 'A History of Western Philosophy'.

My outlook on the world is, like other people's, the product partly of circumstance and partly of temperament. In regard to religious belief, those who were concerned with my education did not, perhaps, adopt the best methods for producing an unquestioning acceptance of orthodoxy. My father and mother were freethinkers, but one of them died when I was two years old and the other when I was three, and I did not know their opinions until I grew up. After my father's death I lived with my grandmother, who was a Scotch Presbyterian but at the age of seventy became converted to Unitarianism. I was taken on alternate Sundays to the parish church (Episcopalian) and to the Presbyterian church, while at home I was instructed in the tenets of the Unitarian faith. I liked the parish church best because there was a comfortable family pew next to the bell rope, and the rope moved up and down all the time the bell was ringing; also because I liked the royal arms which hung on the wall, and the beadle who walked up the steps to the pulpit after the clergyman to close the door upon him at the beginning of the sermon. Moreover, during the service I could study the tables for finding Easter and speculate upon the meaning of Golden Numbers and Sunday Letters and enjoy the pleasure of dividing by ninety, neglecting fractions.

But I was not taught to suppose that everything in the Bible was true, or to believe in miracles and eternal perdition. Darwinism was accepted as a matter of course. I remember a Swiss Protestant tutor, whom I had when I was eleven, saying to me, 'If you are a Darwinian I pity you, for it is impossible to be a Darwinian and a Christian at the same time.' I did not at that age believe in the incompatibility, but I was already certain that if I had to choose, I should choose to be a Darwinian. I continued, however, to believe devoutly in the Unitarian faith until the age of fourteen, at which period I became exceedingly religious and consequently anxious to know whether there was any good ground for supposing religion to be true. For the next four years a great part of my time was spent in secret meditation upon this subject; I could not speak to anybody about it for fear of giving pain. I suffered acutely, both from the gradual loss of faith and from the necessity of silence.

The first dogma which I came to disbelieve was that of free will. It seemed to me that all motions of matter were determined by the laws of dynamics and could not therefore be influenced by the human will, even in the instance of matter forming part of a human body. I had never heard of Cartesianism, or, indeed, of any of the great philosophies, but my thoughts ran spontaneously on Cartesian lines. The next dogma which I began to doubt was that of immortality, but I cannot clearly remember what were at that time my reasons for disbelieving in it. I continued to believe in God until the age of eighteen, since the First Cause argument appeared to me irrefutable. At eighteen, however, the reading of Mill's autobiography showed me the fallacy of this argument. I therefore definitely abandoned all the dogmas of Christianity, and to my surprise I found myself much happier than while I had been struggling to retain some sort of theological belief.

Just after arriving at this stage I went to the University, where for the first time in my life I met people to whom I could speak of matters that interested me. I studied philosophy and under the influence of McTaggart became for a time a Hegelian. This phase lasted about three years and was brought to an end by discussions with G. E. Moore. After leaving Cambridge I spent some years in more or less desultory studies. Two winters in Berlin I devoted mainly to economics. In 1896 I lectured at Johns Hopkins University and Bryn Mawr on non-Euclidean geometry. I spent a good deal of time among art connoisseurs in Florence, while I read Pater and Flaubert and the other gods of the cultured nineties. In the end I settled down in the country with a view to writing a *magnum opus* on the principles of mathematics, which had been my chief ambition ever since the age of eleven.

Indeed, it was at that very early age that one of the decisive experiences of my life occurred. My brother, who was seven years older than I was, undertook to teach me Euclid, and I was overjoyed, for I had been told that Euclid proved things, and I hoped at last to acquire some solid knowledge. I shall never forget my disappointment when I found that Euclid started with axioms. When my brother read the first axiom to me, I said that I saw no reason to admit it; to which he replied that such being the situation we could not go on. Since I was anxious to go on, I admitted it provisionally, but my belief that somewhere in the world solid knowledge was obtainable had received a rude shock.

The desire to discover some really certain knowledge inspired all my work up to the age of thirty-eight. It seemed clear that mathematics had a better claim to be considered knowledge than anything else; therefore it was to the principles of mathematics that I addressed myself. At thirty-eight I felt that I had done all that it lay in my power to do in this field, although I was far from having arrived at any absolute certainty. Indeed, the net result of my work was to throw doubts upon arithmetic which had never been thrown before. I was and am persuaded that the method I pursued brings one nearer to knowledge than any other that is available, but the knowledge it brings is only probable, and not so precise as it appears to be at first sight.

At this point, therefore, my life was rather sharply cut in two. I did not feel inclined to devote myself any longer to abstractions, where I had done what I could without arriving at the desired goal. My mood was not unlike that of Faust at the moment when Mephistopheles first appears to him, but Mephistopheles appeared to me not in the form of a poodle but in the form of the Great War. After Dr. Whitehead and I had finished *Principia Mathematica*, I remained for about three years uncertain what to do. I was teaching in Cambridge, but I did not feel that I wished to go on doing so forever. From sheer inertia I was still occupied mainly with mathematical logic, but I felt – half unconsciously – the desire for some wholly different kind of work.

Then came the war, and I knew without the faintest shadow of doubt what I had to do. I have never been so whole-hearted or so little troubled with hesitation in any work as in the pacifist work that I did during the war. For the first time I found something to do which involved my whole nature. My previous abstract work had left my human interests unsatisfied, and I had allowed them an occasional outlet by political speaking and writing, more particularly on free trade and votes for women. The aristocratic political tradition of the eighteenth and early nineteenth centuries, which I had imbibed in childhood, had made me feel an instinctive responsibility in regard to public affairs. And a strong parental instinct, at that time not satisfied in a personal way, caused me to feel a great indignation at the spectacle of the young men of Europe being deceived and butchered in order to gratify the evil passions of their elders.

Intellectual integrity made it quite impossible for me to accept the war myths of any of the belligerent nations. Indeed, those intellectuals who accepted them were abdicating their functions for the joy of feeling themselves at one with the herd, or in some instances from mere funk. This appeared to me ignoble. *If the intellectual has any function in society, it is to preserve a cool and unbiased judgment in the face of all solicitations to passion.* I found, however, that most intellectuals have no belief in the utility of the intellect except in quiet times.

Again, popular feeling during the war, especially in the first months, afforded me a keen though very painful scientific interest. I observed that at first most of those who stayed at home enjoyed the war, which showed me how much hatred and how little human affection exist in human nature educated on our present lines. I saw also how the ordinary virtues, such as thrift, industry, and public spirit, were used to swell the magnitude of the disaster by producing a greater energy in the work of mutual extermination. I feared that European civilization would perish, as indeed it easily might have done if the war had lasted a year longer. The feeling of security that characterized the nineteenth century perished in the war, but I could not cease to believe in the desirability of the ideals that I previously cherished. Among many of the younger generation, despair has produced cynicism, but for my part I have never felt complete despair and have never ceased, therefore, to believe that the road to a better state of affairs is still open to mankind.

All my thinking on political, sociological, and ethical questions during the last fifteen years has sprung from the impulse which came to me during the first days of the war. I soon became convinced that the study of diplomatic origins, though useful, did not go to the bottom of the matter, since popular passions enthusiastically supported governments in all the steps leading up to the war. I have found myself also unable to accept the view that the origins of wars are always economic, for it was obvious that *most of the people who were enthusiastically in favour of the war were going to lose money by it, and the fact that they themselves did not think so showed that their economic thinking was biased, and that the passion causing the bias was the real source of their warlike feeling.* The supposed economic causes of war, except in the case of certain capitalistic enterprises, are in the nature of a rationalization: *people wish to fight, and they therefore persuade themselves that it is to their interest to do so.* The important question, then, is the psychological one

– 'Why do people wish to fight?' And this leads on from war to a host of other questions concerning impulses to cruelty and oppression in general. *These questions in their turn involve a study of the origins of malevolent passions,* and thence of psychoanalysis and the theory of education.

Gradually, through the investigation of these questions, I have come to a certain philosophy of life, guided always by the desire to *discover some way in which men, with the congenital characteristics which nature has given them, can live together in societies without devoting themselves to making each other miserable.* The keynote of my social philosophy, from a scientific point of view, is the emphasis upon psychology and the practice of judging social institutions by their effects upon human character. During the war all the recognized virtues of sober citizens were turned to a use which I considered bad. Men abstained from alcohol in order to make shells; they worked long hours in order to destroy the kind of society that makes work worth doing. Venereal disease was thought more regrettable than usual because it interfered with the killing of enemies. All this made me acutely aware of the fact that *rules of conduct, whatever they may be, are not sufficient to produce good results unless the ends sought are good.* Sobriety, thrift, industry, and continence, in so far as they existed during the war, merely increased the orgy of destruction. The money spent on drink, on the other hand, saved men's lives, since it was taken away from the making of high explosives.

Being a pacifist forced one into opposition to the whole purpose of the community and made it very difficult to avoid a completely antinomian attitude of hostility to all recognized moral rules. My attitude, however, is not really one of hostility to moral rules; it is essentially that expressed by Saint Paul in the famous passage on charity. I do not always find myself in agreement with that apostle, but on this point my feeling is exactly the same as his – namely, that *no obedience to moral rules can take the place of love, and that where love is genuine, it will, if combined with intelligence, suffice to generate whatever moral rules are necessary.* The word 'love,' however, has become somewhat worn with usage and no longer conveys quite the right shade of meaning. One might start at the other end, from a behaviourist analysis, dividing movements into those of approach and those of withdrawal. In some of the humblest regions of the animal kingdom creatures can be divided, for example, into the phototropic and photophobic – that is, those which approach light and those which fly from it.

The same kind of distinction applies throughout the animal kingdom. In the presence of a new stimulus there may be an impulse of approach or an impulse of retreat. Translated into psychological terms, this may be expressed by saying that there may be an emotion of attraction or an emotion of fear. Both, of course, are necessary for survival, but emotions of fear are very much less necessary for survival in civilized life than they were at earlier stages of human development or among our prehuman ancestors. Before men had adequate weapons, fierce wild beasts must have made life very dangerous, so that men had reason to be as timorous as rabbits are now, and there was an ever-present danger of death by starvation, which has grown enormously less with the creation of modern means of transport.

At the present time the fiercest and most dangerous animal with which human beings have to contend is man, and the dangers arising from purely physical causes have been very rapidly reduced. In the present day, therefore, fear finds little scope except in relation to other human beings, and *fear itself is one of the main reasons why human beings are formidable to each other*. It is a recognized maxim that the best defence is attack; consequently people are continually attacking each other because they expect to be attacked. Our instinctive emotions are those that we have inherited from a much more dangerous world, and contain, therefore, a larger proportion of fear than they should; this fear, since it finds little outlet elsewhere, directs itself against the social environment, producing distrust and hate, envy, malice, and all uncharitableness. If we are to profit fully by our new-won mastery over nature, we must acquire a more lordly psychology: instead of the cringing and resentful terror of the slave, we must learn to feel the calm dignity of the master. Reverting to the impulses of approach and withdrawal, this means that impulses of approach need to be encouraged, and those of withdrawal need to be discouraged. Like everything else, this is a matter of degree. I am not suggesting that people should approach tigers and pythons with friendly feelings; I am only saying that since tradition grew up in a more dangerous world, the present-day occasions for fear and withdrawal are less numerous than tradition would lead us to suppose.

It is the conquest of nature which has made possible a more friendly and co-operative attitude between human beings, and if *rational men co-operated* and used their scientific knowledge to the full, *they could now secure the economic welfare of all* – which was not possible in any earlier period. Life and death competition for the possession of fertile lands was reasonable enough in the past, but it has now become a folly.

International government, business organization, and birth control should make the world comfortable for everybody. I do not say that everybody could be as rich as Crœsus, but *everybody could have as much of this world's goods as is necessary for the happiness of sensible people.* With the problem of poverty and destitution eliminated, men could devote themselves to the constructive arts of civilization – to the progress of science, the diminution of disease, the postponement of death, and the liberation of the impulses that make for joy.

Why do such ideas appear Utopian? The reasons lie solely in human psychology – not in the unalterable parts of human nature, but in those which we acquire from tradition, education, and the example of our environment. Take, first, international government. The necessity for this is patent to every person capable of political thought, but nationalistic passions stand in the way. Each nation is proud of its independence; each nation is willing to fight till the last gasp to preserve its freedom. This, of course, is mere anarchy, and it leads to conditions exactly analogous to those in the feudal ages before the bold, bad barons were forced in the end to submit to the authority of the king. The attitude we have toward foreign nations is one of withdrawal: the foreigner may be all right in his place, but we become filled with alarm at the thought that he may have any say in our affairs. Each state, therefore, insists upon the right of private war. Treaties, arbitration, peace pacts, and the rest are all very well as gestures, but everybody knows that they will not stand any severe strain. So long as each nation has its own army and navy and air force it will use them when it gets excited, whatever treaties its government may have signed.

There will be no safety in the world until men have applied to the rules between different states the great principle which has produced internal security – namely, that *in any dispute, force must not be employed by either interested party but only by a neutral authority after due investigation according to recognized principles of law.* When all the armed forces of the world are controlled by one world-wide authority, we shall have reached the stage in the relation of states which was reached centuries ago in the relations of individuals. Nothing less than this will suffice.

The basis of international anarchy is *men's proneness to fear and hatred.* This is also the basis of economic disputes; for the love of power, which is at their root, is generally an embodiment of fear. Men desire to be in control because they are afraid that the control of others will be used unjustly to their detriment. The same thing applies in the sphere of sexual morals; the power of husbands over wives and of wives over husbands, which is conferred by the law, is derived from fear of the loss of possession. This motive is the negative emotion of jealousy, not the positive emotion of love. In education the same kind of thing occurs. The positive emotion which should supply the motive in education is curiosity, but the curiosity of the young is severely repressed in many directions – sexual, theological, and political. Instead of being encouraged in the practice of free inquiry, children are instructed in some brand of orthodoxy, with the result that unfamiliar ideas inspire them with terror rather than with interest. All these bad results spring from a pursuit of security – a pursuit inspired by irrational fears; the fears have become irrational, since in the modern world fearlessness and intelligence, if embodied in social organization, would in themselves suffice to produce security.

The road to Utopia is clear; *it lies partly through politics and partly through changes in the individal. As for politics, by far the most important thing is the establishment of an international government. As for the individual, the problem is to make him less prone to hatred and fear,* and this is a matter partly physiological and partly psychological. Much of the hatred in the world springs from bad digestion and inadequate functioning of the glands, which is a result of oppression and thwarting in youth. In a world where the health of the young is adequately cared for and their vital impulses are given the utmost scope compatible with their own health and that of their companions, men and women will grow up more courageous and less malevolent than they are at present.

Given such human beings and an international government, the world might become stable and yet civilized, whereas, with our present psychology and political organization, every increase in scientific knowledge brings the destruction of civilization nearer.

Robert Schuller

*N*ow the most conspicuously successful evangelist in America, Dr Robert Schuller began preaching from the roof of a refreshment stand in the 1950s. In the 1970s he built his famous Crystal Cathedral, constructed of clear glass – one of the most audacious and spectacular churches of this century. A master of the media, Schuller turns the latest developments in communications technology to advantage. Advertisements, bestselling books and his T.V. show 'The Hour of Power' make the Crystal Cathedral a dynamo generating Belief on an unprecedented scale. He marries a conservative Protestantism with all the insights of modern psychology to create a challenging, practical approach to Christianity, in which worldly success may be taken as a measure of an individual's contribution to 'the entire human-Divine enterprise'. Robert Schuller speaks for the new, confident Christian, who is determined to turn the tide of scepticism and to set the Church once more in its rightful position of preeminence.

Works include: 'Tough-Minded Faith for Tender Hearted People', 'Tough Times Never Last, But Tough People Do' and 'The Possibility Thinker's Bible'.

I believe in belief. I believe that the human being has the capacity to choose to either believe or doubt! To believe is to make a daring decision before proof of success is possible. I believe that the place of the human being in the universe is established by nature on a belief system. Why, if there is a God in heaven, did He not prove Himself beyond a shadow of a doubt? Why did He leave the ultimate question of His existence and our ability to communicate with Him to the vulnerable human behavioural response we call faith?

If, in fact, God exists, is a knowledge of Him the most important human value? Why did He choose to leave us without positive proof? The answer: We are being 'set up' by our Creator to learn to live by Faith. When proof is possible, then faith is impossible. For no person ever develops as a true person until he learns to make choices. And choices are not choices unless there are debatable options. To choose between alternatives before one can be completely assured which of the two choices is absolutely correct requires a response called 'belief.'

For faith is making a commitment to a position, to a person, to a possibility, before we can be assured that our decision will not prove to be wrong. For this simple reason God has withheld from the human race such proof of His existence, and, therefore, faith becomes necessary as the base of our relationship. Until a person learns to make the right decision – simply because it is the right decision – even before real or fanciful problems are solved – only then will real character be developed. For real character embodies courage. And courage is not the absence of fear. Courage is, in fact, facing a decision that entails enough real risk to frighten one. Thus, more courage lives in time of fear than in times of security. In fact, courage is only possible in the presence and in the face of fear.

The development of faith in the human philosophy of life will result in the emergence of a kind of character that will courageously take a chance in the hope that potential good might be exploited for the benefit of the community of mankind. But such faith cannot be taught. It cannot be genetically transferred from person to person. It must be acquired through personal experience which only comes when we step forward – before we can be sure we will succeed! Only then do we learn the fundamental principle of successful living: 'We will never advance until we take a chance.' So, I believe in faith!

I believe that to have faith in a transcendent God is man's natural and normal mental state that marks him as a mentally and emotionally healthy person. Birds, by nature, belong to the trees and the wind. Fish, in their natural habitat, live and move in the waters. The human being is in his natural habitat and in his highest state of emotional and mental health when he is living and breathing the air of faith. Cynicism, unbelief, or tough skepticism that demands proof for every proposition is neither a mark of intelligence nor emotional health.

I believe in believing! And I believe that if the human being is placed in his natural habitat, faith will naturally be his state of mind. Richard Neutra, the late, great international architect, impressed upon me his doctrine of Bio-Realism. Centrally the principle is this: 'Remove an organism from its natural habitat and its internal guidance system will be distorted and become deviant.'

The human being was designed to live in a garden. The eyes were meant to look upon the changing of the colours from dawn, to dusk, to stars sparkling at night. The ears were designed to pick up the sounds of the garden, the calling of the birds, the whistling of the wind, the rustling of the leaves.

In living and breathing, seeing and sensing, the naked Adam walked in the cool of the garden with sun and breeze brushing the skin and felt a sense of strong spirituality. Tranquillized, experiencing deep relaxation, immune to the type of stress and strain, terror and tension that asphalt jungle human residents experience, the naked human found faith which came naturally and easily. In whatever primitive civilization he found himself religion was instinctive, impulsive, intuitive, incurable!

But removed from the natural habitat, the eyes now convey messages that stimulate the negative emotions. Graphic pictures of violence by one human against another. Power poles that stand on scarred hillsides warn us that if we dare to touch the wires we will burn to a crisp. Sounds of water lapping on soft sands of idyllic beaches are replaced by the mournful wail of sirens and even the crack of gunfire. Loud raucous sounds of discordant melodies amplified unnaturally to irritate the ear drums, compete with the roar of buses and the tension producing jangle of telephones. The smell of the woods and the water and the fragrance of the flowers are replaced by the smell of exhaust fumes vomited in our face by public transportation buses. The human being is out of his natural habitat. The result? An inner tension of which even he is not aware. Except he finds himself pushing and elbowing and shoving his way through the crowds. The quietness and stillness are gone. Secularism and cynicism take their unhealthy and unnatural place to control and dominate life, stifling, if not starving or strangling the human being's healthy inclination to believe in the transcendent God that would speak from the silence.

I believe in belief. It is necessary for human development. It is man's natural destiny!

I believe that God has given us adequate basis for belief. I believe that if there is a God who has created this universe (and more than we will ever know beyond it) then I believe that God is morally obligated to reveal himself to the human being, who is an incurably religious creature.

For, impelled by his instinctive search for meaning, the human being has through his history stumbled and fumbled like a blind man lost in the woods, hoping to satisfy the spiritual passions within himself. Ignorantly, his positive compulsions toward faith have led to an endless array of noble and ignoble attempts to fulfill that natural inner spiritual hunger. Religions have been created out of the starving spiritual needs of primitive persons giving rise to superstitious ritual; anti-human behaviour; to say nothing of wars.

Therefore, I truly believe God had an ethical and a moral obligation to let the human race know the truth about Himself. I believe that He revealed himself to Abraham to be one God! To Moses He revealed a moral code giving rise to ethical monotheism – a religious knowledge of Himself that would establish a base for man's respect for his fellow man. I believe that God further revealed himself through the prophets and finally through Jesus Christ. Ultimately, if God wanted to communicate with a dog He would have had to become a dog. If He wanted to communicate and reveal Himself to the birds, He would have needed to become a bird. He could not escape the holy obligation of becoming a human being – living, breathing, helping, teaching. I believe that God did this once in the body of the human being named Jesus of Nazareth.

I believe truly in the existence of a God of love who encourages us to communicate to him through prayer and assures us that in the power of his Holy Spirit He will give us forgiveness when we penitently seek release from our guilt; He will give us guidance when we seek direction for our daily life; He will send positive thoughts and ideas into our minds that will inspire courage and self confidence.

I believe in the actuality of this God because this was the faith of Jesus of Nazareth. However one interprets the life of Jesus, as a simple human being or as God incarnate and the Messiah promised to ancient Israel – whatever – no one questions the fact that Jesus Himself believed in a God who is personal, intelligent, and all powerful and all loving. 'With men this is impossible, with God all things are possible.' I believe that the life of Jesus was lived with such beauty and nobility and spiritual intelligence that I accept Him and His faith and His opinions on religious matters far more than I trust my own human speculations. Something deep within me would say that it would be the height of arrogance to trust whatever doubts might enter my mind on the existence of God before I would trust the private personal faith of Jesus of Nazareth.

I believe that Jesus claimed to be the incarnation of the eternal God. That He claimed to be God in human flesh. I believe that this act was considered blasphemy in the religious court of His day. I believe that He was brought to trial and given adequate opportunity to clear up the misunderstanding – if that's what the belief in His messiahship was – by His followers or by His enemies. I believe He died personally, wilfully accepting the capital punishment on Him-self to tell the world that He was the son of God! So He died the most shameful and horrific death. And to deny, in the fact of the cross, His deity would be to choose to lie instead of to die.

I believe that He rose again on Easter morning. If in fact He was God in human flesh, – if in fact He was a part of that one God that created this world and had now come to visit it in human flesh, then the miracle is not in His rising from the dead – the real miracle was how could He die completely? And if Christ did not rise from the dead as the early Christians shockingly believed with all their heart and soul, then He was not God in human flesh! And if He was not God, then we are left with the position that God still has not spoken! He has still left us hanging on the bloody edge of impossible human specula-tions. If Christ was not God, – then I do not believe that there is a God at all!

I believe that this Christ somehow used His cruel death in a redemptive way, making possible the elimination of human shame and guilt to all who would embrace Him by faith. I believe that justice and mercy are two of the moral values that are irreconcilable contradictions until we face the cross. I believe God's justice and mercy are combined creatively at the cross of Jesus.

I believe God inflicted upon Himself whatever punishment sinful human beings deserve in a just world. In this one climactic act He has earned enough moral credit to extend that satisfied justice to any human being who begs His mercy and forgiveness. He can now draw from that fathomless reserve of satisfied justice, merciful moral credit to any guilty sinner who asks forgiveness of sins and pardon without having to endure personal punishment! 'Justice and mercy kissed each other on the cross!' So I believe that we are saved from our shame and our guilt through the cross of Jesus Christ.

I believe in salvation now – and forevermore.

I believe in the salvation of the eternal soul. I believe that all human beings are born without faith. I believe that the first stage of child development is the 'learning of trust.' And the absence of trust in the newborn infant is an indication that we are not born believers. Although belief is our natural habitat, we are not born with this faith. We are born with an inclination to be fearful, defensive, and non-trusting. This, I believe, is one of the essential discoveries of Erik Erickson, father of modern child psychiatry. This is the essence of the truth of what theologians have called, for want of a better term, 'original sin.'

I believe that by nature, born without faith, we are all inclined toward a life of fear, suspicion, skepticism, and unbelief until we are 'born again.' Then we are saved from our natural sin of skepticism and unbelief into a life that is structured now with a strong and compulsive and incurable inclination to believe in God, in Christ, in ourselves, and projecting that faith socially in the human race! Then I believe that converted from doubt to faith, from negative thinking to positive thinking, we find our emotional and mental natures tuned to a different wavelength. Different feelings now come over our being. Different ideas enter our minds. And we are knowingly or unknowing living and moving in the stream of Divine Consciousness. We are being God directed and God guided.

Now, glorious possibilities will enter the state of human imagination. We shall find ourselves entertaining high and holy thoughts that are pregnant with potential even though they are surrounded with risk. Quietly we seek guidance; bravely we make the decisions to explore and exploit the positive possibilities even before we can be assured of success. For now the fear of missing a Divine given opportunity outweighs the fear of personal failure. Now we would rather attempt to do something great and fail than attempt to do nothing and succeed. For in this new saving relationship with a heavenly father we come to experience that God's ideas are always humanly impossible. He expects us to begin the God-inspired project before we know all of the answers. It is His way of being a part of the entire human-Divine enterprise. In the process we live on a faith principle. The result? We develop courage! Character! And make great contributions that will translate into social, economic and spiritual progress that all mankind may enjoy the fruits thereof.

And our reward? Our human life's deepest need will be satisfied. We will experience fulfillment! Self-esteem! Self-worth, dignity, and humble pride will be God's blessing given to us. Gone will be the ego drive with all of its demonic dangers and its narcissistic compulsions. In the place of the dangerous egotism there will emerge a handsome, healthy, humble self-esteem! Now saved from doubt, guilt, fear, loneliness we are capable of healthy, interpersonal relationships! Now, we project that Divine Dignity (that falls upon our life as Christians) upon other humans with whom we come in contact treating them with respect even if we don't agree with their ideology, their religious faith, or their unbelieving skeptical secularism.

I believe that human beings cannot long live without bread, water, or air to breath – without the body organism dying. And I believe the spiritual nature of man cannot live long if it has no healthy self esteem. The alternative is shame. And the destructive behaviour of the human being who lives in shame and guilt does not need to be chronicled.

I believe that the salvation of my soul in the here and now results in relief from shame and guilt to self esteem and self confidence! Now great possibilities are generated in the creative mind that has been liberated from the stifling blanket of guilt and personal remorse. And in responding to the dangerous ideas to do God's good work in human society, I will be exercising the ultimate act of repentance and self-denial! I take up my personal cross, paying the price that success always demands! For I believe that true repentance is not an act of self-condemnation. It is rather a constructive and positive laying down of my life to follow the God-inspired call to create a better world for His family of human beings.

And I believe in eternal life. I believe that we all live three lives. The first is nine months in length. How would you communicate to an unborn infant that he is surrounded by flowers, birds, and human beings? How would you communicate to the embryo what sounds and colours are? I believe that after nine months we are born to live a life where a soul evolves and develops. The beginning of the evolution toward spiritual maturity comes when we are challenged to commit ourselves to believe in a God and a spiritual universe before we can be assured that this is Reality. I believe once we make this leap of faith, incredible growth and progress occur within the spiritual consciousness.

I believe that when this life is finished that eternal spiritual quality (we call the soul) that we recognized in human terms as 'imagination,' 'love,' now leaves this organic body like this body left the womb of the mother. We leave the land of the dying to enter the land of the eternal living. I believe that this is a state of eternal existence where our consciousness and awareness transcend our present potential aware-ness and consciousness as the consciousness and awareness of a living human transcends that of an unborn child.

I believe that Jesus knew what was really truth in life here and in the afterlife. And He believed that there would be heaven for those whom God chose to be with Him forevermore. There would be hell for those whom God chose to exclude from His eternal company. For my belief in heaven forces me also to believe in hell. If every soul goes to heaven – then heaven would be a 'hell of a place.' It would cease to be heaven if Adolf Hitler is my unselected and unwelcome room-mate! Integrity is only affirmed in a dialectic situation. 'Yes' has no meaning unless there is a possibility of a 'no!' Love isn't love unless I have the opportunity and the possibility of choosing not to love. Heaven wouldn't be heaven unless there is a contrasting opposite possibility.

I believe that God reserves to Himself the judgment as to who will be in heaven and who will not. I believe that God is free to make that judgment and will be faultless. I believe that any human being can be given assurance of eternal life by accepting sincerely the forgiving friendship and faith of Jesus of Nazareth. For He promised, 'Him that comes unto me I shall in no wise cast out.' (John 6:37)

So I believe in the Gospel of Jesus Christ, 'God so loved the world that He gave his only begotten son that whosoever believe in Him should not perish but have everlasting life.' (John 3:16)

These are my beliefs. I do not claim that it makes me a better person than the one who rejects all or most of my own Christian religion. I do not claim that I am a better person than my unbelieving neighbor. But I do say – and I beg you to believe me – I know better than anyone else that I am a better person because I am a Christian and a believer in this faith – yes, a far better person than I would be if I were not a Christian! For I, better than anyone else, know how often some destructive inclination, some tempting and dehumanizing impulse, some negative or evil mood approached me only to be restrained and rejected by the living Spirit of Jesus that has taken possession of my heart and soul!

Martin Sheen

*T*he most exciting film talent to emerge in the 1970's, Martin Sheen is one of a new breed of thoughtful and caring actors. After a near-fatal heart attack during the filming of 'Apocalypse Now', Sheen realized he was out of touch with his spirit. So began a spiritual quest that ended, during the filming of 'Gandhi' with a return to the Christian faith of his childhood. Now a strong sense of his responsibility to use his influence with the young to good effect has led him to vow never again to play roles which involve killing. He chooses rather to follow the direction of his heart by playing inspired and inspiring men, such as his hero President Kennedy in the recent T.V. biography. 'Acting' he says 'is doing publicly what everyone else does in private'; Sheen's feelings, his outrage at injustice and his love of good, are always exposed, whether on or off the screen. The Director of 'Gandhi', Sir Richard Attenborough, attests that Martin Sheen brings a unique level of sincerity to the parts he plays. The same is true of his writing.

Films include: 'Catch 22', 'Badlands', 'Apocalypse Now', 'Gandhi'.

My father came to America as a young immigrant from Spain in 1918. He had a sixth grade education and could not speak a word of English. He came alone and settled in Dayton, Ohio, where he got a job in the boiler room of a local factory. He learned to speak Italian there so that he could communicate with his fellow workers. There were few other Spaniards in Dayton in 1918 and none working in the boiler rooms of the National Cash Register Company. At night he attended a citizenship school where he met my mother, a fiery young immigrant lass from County Tipperary, Ireland, and they became Americans together as well as partners in life. They raised ten children, nine boys and one girl, before she died in 1951 at the age of 48. He never remarried. I was the seventh son, and suffered from a partially crippling birth defect that caused my father to believe that the only way I could ever succeed in this life was with a college education. This belief was the source of a great deal of friction between us through most of my teenage years because I wanted no part of higher education. For as long as my memory can recall I had always wanted to be an actor, and a college education, so far as I was concerned, was not required; it was a waste of valuable time. I did very poorly in grammar school and beyond. In fact, I had to go to summer school after my senior year in order to earn my High School Diploma. Never the less 'Pop' insisted I go to college, and, since nothing I could do or say would derail his ambition, I arranged to take an entrance examination to the University of Dayton, and promptly failed it on purpose. Out of a possible 100% I scored 3%. That was 25 years ago, and I understand that that score stands to this day as the record low of any entrance exam in the history of the university. Looking back I realize I probably couldn't have done much better if I had really tried. Mind you I'm not at all proud of that distinction, but it helped make the point with my father, who finally saw the wisdom of my view and gave up ever trying to persuade me to do anything else for the rest of his life.

Six months afterwards, when I left home at eighteen to seek a career in the New York Theatre, I went with his full support and blessing, and it remained so until his death in 1974. He was a good and gentle man – he was simple and honest. His name was Francisco Estevez, and he was the best man I ever knew.

The fact is that no one can ever really tell you anything you don't already know – and most of us spend the better part of our lives in a grand celebration of ignorance and folly because we refuse to accept the responsibility for knowing that fact.

Acceptance of responsibility is the true definition of courage, and that's why courage is the first virtue.

The greatness we bear witness to in others is so very often a reflection of the greatness we bear in ourselves. When we negate the recognition of that greatness in our own character, we must compensate by creating heroes elsewhere. We lose the name of action and the very best in us remains dormant and untapped.

Christ himself made direct reference to this phenomena when he rebuked the crowds who were overwhelmed and awed at witnessing his miracles: 'Why are you so amazed?' he said, 'These things you can do and more – you have the power to become sons of God.' Responsibility in its simplest form simply means the ability to respond, and courage is the self-starter.

It is not what we know but what we are willing to learn that is important! And we must begin with self-realization, for the whole universe resides within each one of us individually, and the sun was made to rise and set for a single soul: yours!

The situations facing us at this hour are in essence the very same that faced every prior generation.

That ancient trio and illegitimate offspring of mankind namely, poverty, ignorance and disease are still at large thriving throughout the globe, wreaking havoc, and now those three old bastard hags are sistered to yet another stillborn, illegitimate son: nuclear arms. Together these gangsters form a near complete portrait of the family of man, as they stand posed to let slip the dogs of war and foreclose the future.

I say near complete because a new generation has only now just begun to enter the picture, and to join the many other co-workers in the vineyard near the evening hour. They must not be afraid. They must take courage to enter, for they are not alone.

When asked how she could possibly believe in the goodness and glory or even the existence of a God amidst such horrible poverty and depravation, Mother Teresa replied, 'How can I not? It is far less difficult to deal with the dead and dying in the worst slums of India than it is to deal with the absence of spirituality in America.'

Whether you believe it or not, everything on this planet is precisely as we want it to be consciously or unconsciously, because we are exactly what we want to be personally.

At a final news conference, before he began a long prison sentence for refusal to cooperate with the evils of the Vietnam War and the nuclear arms race, Jesuit Father Daniel Berrigan was confronted by a sarcastic remark: 'Sure Father it's all well and good for you to go to jail for what you believe in – you don't have any children to worry about. What about us? What's going to happen to our children if we go to jail?' To which Father Dan replied, 'What's going to happen to them if you do not?' 'Change,' it has been said, 'Is often desired, frequently necessary and always inevitable.' Your personal fate is inextricably connected to the fate of mankind. The direction of the universe can and will be determined by the presence of individual spirituality or the lack of it. If you would change the world, change yourself and it is done.

As you prepare to embark on your next step of personal endeavor you need only seek the answers to the questions 'Who am I' and 'Why am I here'? and when you arrive at that point where you would not change places with any other living soul, you have begun your journey in earnest.

Be ever mindful that *Truth* never changes – it's only rediscovered!

Be ever mindful that true self love is a virtue devoutly to be wished and that passive self-involvement is a vice to be discarded.

Enter with a measure of optimistic caution but seek them out that call you brother; by their fruits you shall know them;

Enter with *Courage* and never separate strength from compassion.

Enter with *Wisdom* and never separate justice from charity.

Enter with *Joy* and never separate love from labour.

Enter with *Faith* and never separate fact from imagination.

Enter with *Passion* and never separate desire from responsibility.

Enter with *Dignity* and never separate folly from human behaviour.

Enter with *Pride* and never separate humility from achievement.

Enter with *Prudence* and never separate generosity from thrift.

Enter with *Curiosity* and never separate inspiration from potential.

Enter with *Serenity* and never separate laughter from grief.

Enter with *Love* and never separate spirit from flesh.

This, and above all, abandon fear all you who enter here, for you are the children of the universe and you have a right to be where Tagore wished —

Where the mind is clear and the head is held high;

Where knowledge is free;

Where the world has not been broken up into fragments by narrow domestic walls;

Where words come out from the depths of truth;

Where tireless striving stretches its arms towards perfection;

Where the clear stream of reason has not lost its way in the dreary desert sands of dead habit;

Where the mind is led forward by Thee into ever-widening thought and action;

Into that heaven of freedom, my Father, let my country awake!

James Thurber

With his stories of sad little men dreaming of adventure, his provocative vein of misogyny, and his Edward Lear-like drawings, James Thurber is an important commentator on modern life and its morals. The best American humorist since Mark Twain, and the type of the twentieth-century humorous writer, he celebrates stoical resignation and imaginative good humour, the traditional values of comedy, and also tries to cleanse us of the particular forms of self-delusion endemic to our time.

Works include: 'My Life and Hard Times', 'The Middle-Aged Man on the Flying Trapeze' and 'The Secret Life of Walter Mitty'.

Every man is occasionally visited by the suspicion that the planet on which he is riding is not really going anywhere; that the Force which controls its measured eccentricities hasn't got anything special in mind. If he broods upon this sombre theme long enough he gets the doleful idea that the laughing children on a merry-go-round or the thin, fine hands of a lady's watch are revolving more purposefully than he is. These black doubts creep up on a man just before thunderstorms, or at six in the morning when the steam begins to knock solemnly in the pipes, or during his confused wanderings in the forest beyond Euphoria after a long night of drinking.

'Where are we going, if anywhere, and why?' It will do no good to call up *The Times* or consult the *Britannica*. The Answer does not lie in the charts of astronomers or in the equations of mathematicians; it was not indicated by Galileo's swinging lamp or the voices of Joan of Arc; it evaded Socrates and Archimedes and the great men of the Renaissance, and it has evaded everybody else from Francis Bacon to John Kieran. The fearful mystery that lies behind all this endless rotation has led Man into curious indulgences and singular practices, among them love, poetry, intoxicants, religion, and philosophy. Philosophy offers the rather cold consolation that perhaps we and our planet do not actually exist; religion presents the contradictory and scarcely more comforting thought that we exist but that we cannot hope to get anywhere until we cease to exist. Alcohol, in attempting to resolve the contradiction, produces vivid patterns of Truth which vanish like snow in the morning sun and cannot be recalled; the revelations of poetry are as wonderful as a comet in the skies, and as mysterious. Love, which was once believed to contain the Answer, we now know to be nothing more than an inherited behaviour pattern.

Before we can pronounce any judgment on Man's destiny, we must take a look at the dilemma into which he has got himself. We must examine his nature before we can measure his hope of Heaven. For some curious reason Man has always assumed that his is the highest form of life in the universe. There is, of course, nothing at all with which to sustain this view. Man is simply the highest form of life on his own planet. His superiority rests on a thin and chancey basis: he had the trick of articulate speech and out of this, slowly and laboriously, he developed the capacity of abstract reasoning. Abstract reasoning in itself, has not benefited Man so much as instinct has benefited the lower animals. On the contrary, it has moved in the opposite direction. Instinct has been defined as 'a tendency to actions which lead to the attainment of some goal natural to the species.' In giving up instinct and going in for reasoning, Man has aspired higher than the attainment of natural goals; he has developed ideas and notions; he has monkeyed around with concepts. The life to which he was naturally adapted he has put behind him; in moving into the alien and complicated sphere of Thought and Imagination he has become the least well-adjusted of all the creatures of the earth, and hence the most bewildered. It may be that the finer mysteries of life and death can be comprehended only through pure instinct; the cat, for example, appears to Know (I don't say that he does, but he appears to). Man, on the other hand, is surely farther away from the Answer than any other animal this side of the ladybug. His mistaken selection of reasoning as an instrument of perception has put him into a fine quandary.

The survival of almost any species of social animal, no matter how low, has been shown to be dependent on Group Co-operation, which is itself a product of instinct. Man's co-operative processes are jumpy, incomplete, and temporary because they are the product of reasoning and are thus divorced from the sanity which informs all natural laws. The lower animals co-operate in the interest of the preservation of their species. Man no longer has the natural, earthly sense which would interest him in the preservation of his species. The co-operation of the lower social animals is constructive, that of man destructive. 'Group struggles to the death between animals of the same species, such as occur in human warfare, can hardly be found among non-human animals,' says W. C. Allee in his enormously interesting *The Social Life of Animals.*

The animals that depend upon instinct have an inherent knowledge of the laws of economics and of how to apply them; Man with his powers of reason has reduced economics to the level of a farce which is at once funnier and more tragic than *Tobacco Road.* One has but to observe a community of beavers at work in a stream to understand the loss in sagacity, balance, co-operation, competence, and purpose which Man has suffered since he rose up on his hind legs. His grip on the earth and its realities began to lessen in that hour; he could walk, but he had lost the opposability of his hallux, and his feet were no longer prehensile. Two of his parts increased enormously in size: his gluteus maximus and his cerebrum. He began to chatter and he developed Reason, Thought, and Imagination, qualities which would get the smartest group of rabbits or orioles in the world into inextricable trouble overnight. Man, the aloof animal, has deteriorated in everything except mentality and in that he has done no more than barely hold his own for the past two thousand years. He no longer understands the ways of the lower animals and they no longer understand the ways of Man. Here again it is Man that has suffered the loss.

Next to reasoning, the greatest handicap to the optimum development of Man lies in the fact that his planet is just barely habitable. Its minimum temperatures are too low and its maximum temperatures are too high. Its day is not long enough and its night is too long. The disposition of its water and its earth is distinctly unfortunate (the existence of the Mediterranean Sea in the place where we find it is perhaps the unhappiest accident in the whole firmament). These factors encourage depression, fear, war, and lack of vitality. They describe a planet which is by no means perfectly devised for the nurturing, or for the perpetuation, of a higher intelligence. The effect of all this on Man is everywhere apparent. On his misfit globe he has outlasted the mammoth and the pterodactyl, but he has never got the upper hand of bacteria and the insects. 'This is not even the age of Man, however great his superiority in size and intelligence,' writes Mr. Allee, 'it is literally the age of insects.' It is surely not going too far, in view of everything, to venture the opinion that Man is not so high as he thinks he is. It is surely permissible to hazard the guess that somewhere beyond Betelgeuse there may be a race of men whose intelligence makes ours seem like the works of an old-fashioned music box. The Earth, it seems to me, may well be the Siberia, or the Perth Amboy, of the inhabited planets of the Universe.

Now that we have got Man down on his back, so to speak, let us look at the tongue of his intellect and feel the pulse of his soul. There is a great deal to be said for his intellect, in spite of the fact that it is unquestionably coated. It has produced Genius and out of Genius has come Art, the one achievement of Man which has made the long trip

107

up from all fours seem well-advised. Most of the faint intimations of immortality of which we are occasionally aware would seem to arise out of Art, or the materials of Art. This brings us to God and Heaven, the last stop which this exploration into the known and the unknown will make.

Everybody is supposed to have some opinion as to whether there is life after death. Intelligent persons are expected to formulate 'an integrated and consistent attitude toward life or reality'; this is known as 'a philosophy' (definition 2c in *Webster's New International Dictionary*). Unfortunately, I have never been able to maintain a consistent attitude toward life or reality, or toward anything else. This may be entirely due to nervousness.At any rate, my attitudes change with the years, sometimes with the hours. Just now I am going through one of those periods when I believe that the black panther and the cedar waxwing have a higher hope of Heaven than Man has. The Dignity of Man and the Divine Destiny of Man are two things which it is at the moment impossible for me to accept with wholehearted enthusiasm. Human Dignity has gleamed only now and then and here and there, in lonely splendour, throughout the ages, a hope of the better men, never an achievement of the majority. That which is only sporadically realized can scarcely be called characteristic. It is impossible to think of it as innate, it could never be defined as normal. Nothing is more depressing than the realization that nobility, courage, mercy, and almost all the other virtues which go to make up the ideal of Human Dignity, are, at their clearest and realest, the outgrowth of Man's inhumanity to Man, the fruit of his unending interspecific struggle. The pattern is easily traceable, from Christ to Cavell.

In spite of everything, it is perhaps too easy to figure Man as merely an animal of the earth whose cerebrum developed extraordinarily, like the peacock's tail or the giraffe's neck, and to let it go at that. There is always Browning's 'plaguey hundredth chance' that the mysterious inner eye which seems to see God, actually does see God; and that God sees it, too. There is always Browning's 'grand Perhaps.' If it is hard to Believe, it is just as hard, as our poet's Bishop Blougram points out to the cynical Mr. Gigadibs, to 'guard our unbelief.' You remember: 'Just when we are safest, there's a sunset-touch, a fancy from a flower-bell' and all that sort of thing – and we believe again. And then there's a man with a little moustache, and a man with an umbrella, and all *that* sort of thing, and we are safe once more in our conviction that there can be no God watching over this sorrowful and sinister scene, these menacing and meaningless animals.

We come back, in the end, to all that we can safely feel we know: a monkey man in the Eolithic times, wandering through the jungle, came upon a jewel and stuck it into his head. Since that day his descendants have given off light, sometimes a magic and blinding light. The question whether the jewel was carelessly flung off from a whirling star or carefully planned and placed by a supernatural hand has engaged the interest of mankind for a million years. The question will go on and on: is this light a proof of God or is it no more remarkable than the plumage of a bird of paradise?

'Come, come, it's best believing, if we can,' says the jovial Sylvester Blougram, over his wine. 'Why not,' he asks, ' "the Way, the Truth, the Life?" ' Why not, indeed? It is all right with me, I say over my own wine. But what is all this fear of, and opposition to, Oblivion? What is the matter with the soft Darkness, the Dreamless Sleep? 'Well, folks,' the cheery guard may say, as the train rushes silently into a warm, dark tunnel and stops, 'Here we are at good old Oblivion! Everybody out!' Come, come, what is the matter with that? I ask – over my scotch and soda.

H. G. Wells

A literary and philosophical adventurer, H. G. Wells loved ideas with an unparalleled enthusiasm. The first great novelist with a scientific training, he was one of the inventors and masters of science fiction, accurately predicting, among other things, the nuclear bomb. He was an innovator in many areas of thought, advocating free-love, feminism and a sort of aristocracy of the mind and spirit to replace that of birth and money. Seeing himself as a 'cosmic doctor,' he wanted to liberate people from outmoded conventions and to shock them into coming to terms with the neuroses of the age.

Works include: 'The Time Machine', 'The War of the Worlds', 'Kipps' and 'The History of Mr Polly'.

It has exercised my mind a lot to find out how much I could tell you of my credo in a few thousand words or so. Because I suppose that means telling what I think I am, why I exist, what I think I am for, what I think of life, what I think of the world about me, and things like that. These are questions to which I have given innumerable hours – in conversation, in reading and writing, in lonely places, and particularly in that loneliest place of all, the dark stillness of the night. Anyhow I am going to try.

In the perfume factories of Grasse, in Provence, they show you little bottles of concentrated extract. In this little bottle, they tell you, they have condensed the scent of half a million roses; in this, acres and acres of jasmine. In this brief paper I shall try to give you the gist of thousands of nights and days of thought. I shall try to make myself as clear as possible, but you must forgive me if now and then I have to be more concentrated than explicit.

I can say best what I have to say by talking first about immortality. I shall open my matter with a question. Here I am, setting down my thoughts; and there you are, reading them. We are having mental intercourse, sharing our ideas. Our mental lives are in contact. The question I would put is this: how far can we consider this mental life we are sharing to be immortal? And more particularly I would ask you a question I have often asked myself. What is this H. G. Wells who is now thinking before you and with you?

Now what do you suppose our little conference amounts to? What is happening now? You are Mr So-and-so, or Mrs So-and-so, or Miss So-and-so and someone called H. G. Wells is talking to you through the medium of print. That is what most people will call self-evident fact. That is what will pass muster as the truth of the matter. But is it altogether true? Let us go into things a little more precisely. I will talk about my side of the discussion, which is H. G. Wells, but what I have to say will apply quite as well to your side also.

This H. G. Wells is a visible tangible human being who was born in the year 1866 and who has since gone here and there and done this and that. His words are here, some thought that may be considered to be his is here, but are you sure that all of him is present? May I point out that, far from all of him being present in this discussion, very much of him is not present anywhere. The greater part of him is no longer in existence. It is dead. It is past and largely forgotten. He is already, for the most part, as dead as his grandfather.

Let me explain a little more fully what I mean by this. Consider the childhood of this human being. I will tell you of one incident in it. In 1867 he was a small and extremely troublesome infant. He felt things vividly and expressed himself violently. He had, one day, a great and terrible adventure. It must have seemed like the end of the world to him. He was lying on a sofa and he rolled about upon it and fell off. He must have been scared by that fall. But also he fell on a glass bottle. It broke. He was cut very dreadfully about the face. This body I have with me to-day still bears a scar over one eye. No doubt he was frightened and hurt, taken up and soothed. The doctor came and sewed him up.

What a storm of feeling, what a fuss it must have been! Yes, but what do I know of all that now? Nothing, nothing whatever except what my mother told me of it; nothing else at all. All the fear, all the feeling, all the details of the event have gone out of my conscious existence. All that is quite dead. Now, can I really say that H. G. Wells of one year old is here? You will say, perhaps, 'Of course he is.' There is the scar. And if that child of twelve months old had not existed, how could this present writer exist!

But wait a moment. That grandfather of mine! He was a gardener and he was rather good at growing roses. One day toward the end of the reign of King George III he stood in the sunshine in a garden at Penshurst and budded a rose. I know that for a fact, just as completely as I know for a fact that H. G. Wells fell off a sofa in 1867. And also, be it noted, if my grandfather had not existed, the present writer could not exist. My nose and my eyes would not be the shape and colour they are. If the scar is H. G. Wells of 1867, the eye is Joseph Wells of 1828. So, by the same test, if that infant H. G. Wells is alive here, his grandfather is alive here, and so far as one is dead and forgotten, so is the other. There is the same physical continuity; there is the same forgetfulness.

Now this idea that the H. G. Wells who writes this is not all of H. G. Wells is a very important idea in my credo. It is not only that I who am speaking am not in any real sense that baby of 1867, but it is also that I am not a certain ill and angry young man of twenty who lived in 1886. He was struggling in the world under what he thought was an unjustly heavy handicap, and he talked and he wrote. I have photographs of him as he was then; I have stuff that he wrote. And for the life of me I cannot identify my present self with him. I have left him behind almost as completely as I have left my grandfather behind. On the other hand, I have been recently collaborating with one of my sons. We share many ideas and we have very similar mental dispositions. I feel at present much more closely identified with him than with that young H. G. Wells of 1886: or even with the H. G. Wells of 1896, who I find from a photograph wore side whiskers and a cascade moustache and rode about the countryside on a bicycle. I don't remember ever looking at those moustache and side whiskers in a looking-glass. If it were not for the photograph I could easily have denied that moustache.

And now let us turn to another aspect of this curious inquiry. This train of thought which is talking to you now is something very much less than H. G. Wells, who is, from my point of view, already very largely dead. But it is also something very much *more* than H. G. Wells. You and I are thinking whether there is anything immortal in ourselves. Now H. G. Wells never started that topic. It came to him. He heard people talking about it and preaching about it. He read about it. People who died in Egypt five thousand years ago and whose names and faces and habits are utterly forgotten were talking about it. Plato, Buddha, Confucius, St. Paul have all had something important to say on the matter. That discussion came into *our* lives as we grew up. We may participate in it, change it a little, before we pass it on. It is like a light passing through a prism which may test it, refract it perhaps, polarize it perhaps, and send it on again *changed*. We are so to speak prisms. The thoughts existed before we were born and will go on after we have been finished with altogether.

Now here, you see, is something more – and something very fundamental – of what I am trying to say to you. Either this will seem the most lucid of realities or the most fantastic of speculations. But first let us have what I am putting to you plain. Here, I say, is this H. G. Wells who is talking, and he is – I have tried to show – so far from being immortal that the greater part of him is already dead and gone forever. I will not presume to apply the obvious parallel to you. That is your affair. But also over and above this H. G. Wells is something, a living growth and a continual refining of ideas, a thought process which is bringing our minds together. And this thought process has lived already thousands of years ago and may, so far as we know, passing from mind to mind and from age to age, continue its life forever. We are mortal persons responding to the advance of perhaps immortal ideas. We are not ourselves only; we are also part of human experience and thought.

I hope I have made my meaning clear thus far. You may not agree with me exactly, but I hope you have understood me, so that I can go on to the next article in my credo.

A second very fundamental question which man has been debating with himself for many centuries, and which comes to most of us in due time and perplexes us, is the question of what is an individual. It is a question that joins on very closely to these ideas about immortality. How is the individual related to the species? How is the part related to the whole? How is the one related to the many? How is he or she as a whole related to everything in his or her make-up? A great part of the dialogues of Plato, for instance, consists of experiments and explorations about this group of questions. The controversies of the Schoolmen centred upon it. Our modern professors of philosophy do not attach sufficient importance to the issues between the Nominalists and the Realists. They were of fundamental importance.

I agree that to a lot of people this sort of discussion will seem hairsplitting, tedious, and unmeaning. They will fail to see what it is about and what good it is. They feel sure they are individuals, and that is an end to the matter. They will say that they do not want to bother their heads about it. Quite a lot of people seem to live now chiefly to escape having their heads bothered about anything, but most of that kind have probably stopped reading this a while ago, if ever they began. To many, however, these questions are full of meaning, and to some of us they are among the most important questions in the world. They are so to me, and I cannot explain what I believe at all without discussing them.

I suppose the ordinary and obvious answer to this question of what is an individual would be to say it is a living being detached from the rest of the world. It is born or hatched as a definite, distinctive body; it maintains itself for a certain time against the rest of the universe, and at last it dies and comes to a physical end. But is that an impregnable statement? If one pries into descriptive biology or into modern psychology, one finds first one curious fact and then another coming up to weaken and undermine this idea of the complete integrity of individuals. They are not so definitely marked off as we are to think.

Go first to the biologist. He will agree that men and cats and dogs are very individual creatures. He will probably say that they are strongly individualized. But when you ask him if that is true of all living things, he will at once say, 'No.' He will tell you that most plants seem much more individualized than they are. You can take a plant and break it up into a number of plants. Are they new individuals or are they fractions of the old one? You can even take two plants of different species and graft them together. What is the grafted plant – a new individual, or one or both of the old ones? Trees seem to be much more individual than they really are, just as mountains do. It is a disposition of our minds to think of them as individuals. We talk of the Jungfrau or the Wetterhorn as if they were as complete and distinct as pyramids, but really they are only outstanding peaks on a general mountain mass.

And it is not only the vegetable kingdom that is wanting in distinct individuality. The biologist will tell you of innumerable species of lower animals also, of which two sometimes come together and coalesce into one and one will break up into two or many; and again of individuals that branch off others but never separate and so become what are called colonies, a sort of superindividual. If the higher animals could do as the lower animals do, we should have Herr Hitler coalescing with Mr. Stalin into one individual to the great dismay of the Anti-Comintern – and we should have Mr. Winston Churchill breaking up into dozens and scores of Winston Churchills, and writing books, painting pictures, forming governments, commanding and constituting armies and navies, and carrying every aspect of his versatility to the last extreme. I am afraid he would insist upon it.

But the biologist assures us that all the higher animals have lost their powers of combining and dividing and spreading themselves out. They are highly individualized, he says; they are unified and drawn together, they are cut off from the rest of the universe and concentrated in their bodies, to a degree no other creatures have attained. These individualities such as we human beings possess are an exception and not the rule among living things. They are not the common fashion of life.

But though we are highly individualized, says the biologist, our kind of creature is not completely individualized. He will tell you of various curious cases when sheep and cats and dogs and babies have been born with two heads to one body or two bodies to one head. When there are two heads, where is the individual then? And he will bring home to you the fact that a great part of our bodily selves is unknown to us. We do not even know what is inside these bodies of ours until we learn about it from talk and lessons and books, and unless trouble is brewing we do not know what goes on inside there nor how it feels. Our particular individuality, in fact, does not penetrate to our interiors.

And if you will let the biologist run on, he will tell you that in the blood vessels and substance of our body are millions of little beings, which are extraordinarily like some of the smallest, lowest microscopic animals which lead independent lives, and these go about in our bodies as citizens go about in the streets and houses of a city. These little beings, these corpuscles, kill disease germs, carry food and air about, and do a multitude of services. They have minute individualities of their own. We are made up of millions of such minute creatures, just as cities and nations are made of millions of such beings as ourselves. There are, you see, different ranks and kinds of individuality. It is not the simple matter so many people assume it to be.

Now when we turn from the modern biologist to the modern psychologist, we get still more remarkable revelations about this individuality of ours, which seems at first so simple. He tells us of minds split and divided against themselves. I do not know whether you have read of cases of what is called divided personality. They are fascinatingly strange. They are rare, but they occur. There are people who suddenly forget who they are. The ordinary personality gives place to a different one. That may happen under hypnotism; it may happen in cases of insanity.

But it may also happen without either hypnotism or insanity. In the same brain and in the same body it is possible for first one and then another personality to take control. Perhaps you have read a story of R. L. Stevenson's which was suggested by these cases – the story of *Dr. Jekyll and Mr. Hyde*. That puts these phenomena in an extreme, fantastic fashion, and it ascribes the change-over to a drug. But the change in the actual cases occurs without a drug. Quite a number of us go some little way toward such a change. Which of us, indeed, has not a better self and a worse self?

I am making this appeal to biology and psychology as brief as possible, but I think I have at least said enough to show you the support I find in these sciences for my profound doubt whether this H. G. Wells of mine is really the completely independent, separate, distinct being that it is our habit of mind to consider him. Perhaps my individuality, my personality, seems to be distincter than it is. Perhaps it is – how shall I put it? – a convenient biological illusion.

I could produce a great mass of facts to support that belief, to show how individuality has arisen in the course of evolution and how every individual is, as it were, a sort of experiment made by nature to test this and that group of qualities. In collaboration with Julian Huxley and my son, G. P. Wells, I have been trying to present that mass of facts to the general reader in a work called *The Science of Life*, but our utmost efforts to compress and simplify leave us with a large book. So I can only allude to it here as being full of light upon this issue, the sort of light there is no time to give you now, and then turn to another aspect of this question of 'What am I?' and 'What are you?'

Let us look within. How do you feel about your identity with yourself? Well, anyhow, let me tell you how *I* feel about H. G. Wells. I have already tried to show that as a matter of fact a lot of him is already dead stuff and irrelevant stuff, and I have also tried to show that this *thought* that is talking to you is something very much more than H. G. Wells.

And when it comes to introspection, then I feel, very, very clearly, that I am something very distinct from this individual H. G. Wells who eats and sleeps and runs about the world. I feel that I am linked to him as a boat may be moored to a floating buoy. More than this, I have to use his voice, see with his eyes, experience the pain of any physical misfortune that comes to him. He is my window on the world and my mouthpiece. I have to think in his brain, and his store of memories is my only reference library. I doubt if I can think or feel or act as an individual without him. But I do not feel that I am he.

I take a great interest in him. I keep him as clean as I can and am always on the watch to prevent him getting sulky, dull, or lazy – not always with success. He has to be petted and persuaded. I like to be told he is good and remarkable, just as I like to be told my automobile is a good one. But sometimes I wish I could get away from him – heavens, how I wish it at times! He is clumsy in all sorts of ways, and unbeautiful. Some of his instincts and appetites are dreadful. He begins to show considerable signs of wear. The reference library in him might be better arranged and the brain cells quicker on the uptake. But he is all I have to keep me in touch with the world. When he goes, I believe that I shall go. I shall be silenced for ever.

Now there is nothing original in this sense of detachment from myself. Most people get to something of the sort. When we are young, we identify ourselves with ourselves very completely and fiercely. That may be a biological necessity. But as we ripen – or as we age – the separation widens. All through the historical past of our race one can trace this feeling of detachment. They used to call the part that is talking to you now the soul, and the rejected part the body; but that is not quite my point of view.

The H. G. Wells I look down upon is mental just as much as he is physical; he is the whole individualized, self-centred personality. When I read St. Paul and find him talking of the Old Adam and the New Adam, he seems to be saying something very much nearer to the truth than that popular distinction of body and spirit. When he cries, 'Who can deliver me from the body of this death?' I find him very understandable. How warmly have I echoed that cry! My feeling is just that sense of being *thought* – a part of a great process of thought – which finds itself entangled, as some young creature may be entangled in its egg membranes, in an overdeveloped, overintense, overlimited egotism.

Now what I am saying here is not, I believe, an orthodox Christian view. Orthodox Christianity insists that we are ourselves forever and ever. My credo is much nearer Stoicism. It is, indeed, Stoicism seen in the light of modern biological science. I do not believe in the least that either the body of H. G. Wells or his personality is immortal, but I do believe that the growing process of thought, knowledge, and will of which we are parts, of which I am a part, and of which you are a part, may go on growing in range and power without limit. I think that Man may be immortal, but not men.

There you have what I believe about myself, given to you as precisely and clearly as I can. Man, I take it – Man in us – is more important than the things in the individual life, and this I believe not as a mere sentimentality, but as a rigorously true statement of biological and mental fact. Our individuality is, so to speak, an inborn obsession from which we shall escape as we become more intelligent. And we are under a necessity to escape from it as we become more intelligent, because increasing intelligence brings us more and more clearly face to face with the ultimate frustration of every individual desire in age, enfeeblement, and death. Personality, individuality, may be a biological device which has served its end in evolution and will decline. A consciousness of something greater than ourselves – the immortal soul of the race – may be taking control of the direction of our lives.

If I had the time and erudition, I think I could make an argument to show that this idea of the immortal soul of the race in which our lives are like passing thoughts, is to be found in what Confucius called the Higher Person, in what St. Paul called the New Adam, in the Logos of Stoics, in the modern talk we hear of the Overman or Superman. But I cannot pursue these suggestions now.

But if I might say a word or so about the views one gets from this credo, I should insist first that the subordination of self to a higher order of being does not mean the suppression of all or any of one's distinctive gifts. We have to use ourselves to the utmost. We have to learn and make to the full measure of our possibilities. It is a sin to bury the talent, the individual gift which we possess for the good of the greater being, Man.

Nor must you imagine that the subordination of self to the immortal being of the race means a subordination of one's narrow self to the equally narrow selves of other people. It is for them also to give themselves to that life and all that increases knowledge and power. I do not believe in the surrender of one jot or one tittle of one's intelligence and will to the greatest happiness of the greatest number, or to the will of the majority, or any such nonsense: I am not that sort of democrat. This world and its future is not for feeble folk any more than it is for selfish folk. It is not for the multitude, but for the best. The best of to-day will be the commonplace of to-morrow.

If I am something of a social leveller, it is not because I want to give silly people a good time, but because I want to make opportunity universal, and not leave out one single being who is worth while. If I want economic change, it is because the present system protects and fosters a vast swarm of wasteful spenders, no better in their quality and much worse in their lazy pretentious traditions than the general run of mankind. If I am opposed to nationalism and war, it is not merely because these things represent an immense waste of energy, but because they sustain a cant of blind discipline and loyalty and a paraphernalia of flags, uniforms, and parades that shelter a host of particularly mischievous, unintelligent bullies and wasters; because they place our lives at the mercy of trained blockheads. Militarism and warfare would be childish things, if they were not more horrible than anything childish can be. They must become things of the past.

They must die. Naturally my idea of politics is an open conspiracy to hurry these tiresome, wasteful, evil things – nationality and war – out of existence; to end this empire and that empire, and set up the one Empire of Man.

And it is natural that I should exalt that continual process of questioning which we call science. In the scientific world I find just that disinterested devotion to great ends that I hope will spread at last through the entire range of human activity. I find just that co-operation of men of every race and colour to increase Man's knowledge. We can all be citizens of the free state of science. But our political, our economic, our social lives have still to become illuminated and directed by the scientific spirit, are still sick and feeble with congenital traditionalism.

A page or so before this, I have written 'Man "may be" immortal.' When first I wrote this credo I wrote with more confidence, 'is immortal.' Since then I have scrutinized the possible *Fate of Man* more narrowly, and I have replaced my certitude by a more cautious statement. I realize more clearly than I did that Man's future is conditional upon his foresight and his ability to face the changing conditions of life about him. The world has plainly become much darker and more dangerous. Open free speech has ceased over vast areas. There has been much promiscuous killing, much waste of natural resources and much economic disorganization. Violence has made headway against the world's peace, and the level of civilized life is visibly sinking. The element of hope many of us entertained for a new way of living in Soviet Russia has dwindled, almost to nothing. The call for positive activities to arrest the decay is much more urgent than it was. A few years ago one could write 'I am opposed to nationalism and war' and 'I exalt science' and leave it at that. Now that does not satisfy. How long shall I be free to maintain these excellent attitudes if I do not exert myself to defend them? The political end of one's philosophy now, has to be of a more practical quality. The question of 'What are you going to do about it?' is more urgent.

It no longer suffices merely to disapprove of war and of the freedom of egotistical recklessness in the private exploitation of natural resources. The call to immediate action requires a plan for immediate action. We need a working estimate of the disorders we have to face. Certain facts now stare us in the face. All war is not nationalist; abolish nationalist sovereignty and there would still be a social war on hand. Moreover war changes its physical conditions and material effects monstrously, and so it follows that a philosophy which professes to be living must be prepared to state what it is that has so greatly exacerbated the war danger. I find the answer to that inquiry, in a great release of human energy and a rapid dissolution of social classes, through the ever-increasing efficiency of economic organization and the utilization of mechanical power. As machinery and the material organization of life has improved, social order has become deliquescent.

Let me put this idea as plainly as possible. Throughout the ages the processes of social life have been carried on by long-established and well-defined classes, professions and types of functionary, priest, soldier, lawyer, artisan, merchant, peasant. They had all, in effect, time-sanctioned codes of behaviour, codes that were almost universally understood and respected. A sort of rough social balance among these elements had stood the tests of several thousand years. There was balance during that period even in the structure and method of armies and the conduct of war, with cavalry, infantry, and an accessory artillery. Life adapted itself gradually to such gradual changes as were in progress. Gunpowder, for instance, was a small slow innovation compared with the aeroplane and the tank. Then suddenly came the onset of power machinery and a new scale of human operations. New wholesale mechanical methods, transport of commodities, gas, explosives and so forth, have not only made war an entirely different and more catastrophic thing but – what is not so universally recognized – they have twisted the old functional classifications of mankind in peace or war almost out of recognition. We did not realize what was happening until quite recently, and we are still trying to run a new and imperfectly understood machinery of living, with the traditions, feelings, sentiments, morality, culture, of the time-honoured old order.

These traditions, almost all of them over-implemented now and many of them now plainly mischievous or reduced to utter futility, tangle us into the most alarming and sanguinary strains and stresses. Old classes change or vanish; new ones appear. The old-fashioned farmer who satisfied most of his needs by his own products, has vanished over great parts of the world and we call the new crop-grower by his name and judge him by bucolic precedents. Really he has been as much industrialized as any factory hand. Formerly he grew food and material for clothing and little else. Now he grows also a vast variety of raw materials for chemical use in industry. Continually our productive efficiency increases and everywhere our new productions so outstrip our old traditions of financial control and marketing control that a new, hitherto unheard-of stratum of able-bodied, unemployed, untrained, and aimless young men appears. We get them in great multitudes, and our methods of distributing the products of industry, neither employ nor satisfy nor dispose of them. What are we to do with them?

All the civilized communities suffer from a sort of cancer of irrelevant, useless, energetic young people. Their lack of function is a purely disintegrating force. We seem to have no better employment for them than to turn them over to war-preparation, which must lead at last to their consumption in war. Human life has stalled; its organization has clogged with a growing surplus of human beings it can neither interest nor use. And this surplus energy produces violence and incoherent instinctive revolutionary movements of increasing gravity.

This condition of things was unanticipated. In three or four decades it has rushed upon us and become the major problem of the reclassification of society, and the reorientation of humanity to a new, vaster, richer and more satisfying set of objectives, has to be tackled strenuously and immediately. It tolerates no philosophical aloofness. It towers over us all, a stupendous menace. Only an enormous intellectual effort throughout the whole world, can arrest this headlong deliquescence of human society that is now in progress. So that for my own part I have become a shouting philosopher and I clamour, and I clamour with an increasing shrillness for a gigantic effort to pull together the mind of the race before it is altogether too late. 'Adapt,' I say, 'let us adapt ourselves to these greater demands, or Man must perish and our faith is vain.'

And it is because we do not know how to adapt, because of our lack of exactitude and coordination, that this necessity to inquire, to think hard, to accumulate the definite will for a new order, assumes an almost passionate predominance in my thoughts. Study, clarify, educate, without panic indeed but without a moment's delay, interchange and speak plainly, this must surely be the primary rule of life for every rational man and woman to-day. The hour is late, but still amidst the deepening shadows we may be in time. Build up an acceptable vision of a new world, make, not a flimsy gesture of good intentions, but work, work hard, to produce a reasoned and tried and tested common plan that will hold human minds together in a new order in the world. So I say and repeat, first in one form and then in another, that an educational revolution, a new encyclopaedism, a new mental synthesis, must be the basis of any better life, and that failing that, humanity must perish. At present all our efforts to produce a new human society are insufficiently implemented with knowledge. More science is needed, more interchange and more co-ordination. Act to that end. This is my philosophy of action; this is my philosophy of myself as a living part of Man, brought now by the danger of his ultimate failure to a cutting edge.

Such in brief is my credo. I hope I have interested you and I hope I have not offended you. This is how I am living and how I hope to live to my end.

It has been good to be a part of life. Just as a sundial counts only the sunny hours, so does life know only that it is living. Many experiences there are in life, but one there is that we shall never have. We shall never know that we are dead. And I shall be fighting until I am dead. My creed, I can assure you, is not an unhappy creed. I have found it a good working creed, and at the most desperate an exciting one.

Rebecca West

*O*ne of the founding mothers of modern feminism, Rebecca West showed both in her work and her life an insight into human nature of extraordinary depth and individuality. Her absolute belief in the Augustan doctrine of original sin led her to understand man as a hating rather than as a loving animal. Her view was that we ought to pursue pleasure but that we generally find it easier to court pain. Forthright and abrasive she wrote as she lived, fiercely and with a reckless intensity.

Works include: 'The Return of the Soldier', 'The Climate of Treason' and 'The Birds Fall Down'.

I have no faith in the sense of comforting beliefs which persuade me that all my troubles are blessings in disguise. I do not believe that any facts exist, or, rather, are accessible to me, which give any assurance that my life has served an eternal purpose. I do not find this distressing. That is not because my life has been so happy that its superficial import strikes me as satisfactory. My childhood and my girlhood were overshadowed by the tragedies of my elders, and my twenties were a nightmare of overwork and harassment. Not till my marriage – and I married in my late thirties – did I have one human being close to me who ever thought seriously of saving me fatigue or pain or responsibility. There have been many worse fates than mine; but I cannot think it ideal.

Nevertheless, I feel no overwhelming anxiety to find some creed to assure me that all has been for the best, which will tell me that I have only to follow a particular path to be consoled by eternal happiness. It may be that I should feel such anxiety if I were stricken by a painful and incurable disease, but as yet I have not felt it. I do not even find in myself any great curiosity as to whether my soul is immortal or not. If I received definite and convincing information either way I should certainly be very interested, though not, I think, either extremely depressed or elated; but I do not feel the lack of such information as a hardship.

The real interest of the universe seems to me not to lie in these directions at all. The reason I feel no hunger for a creed that shall reveal to me the secret of the universe is that I do not see how the existence of such a creed is compatible with the condition of humanity. I cannot understand how our minds, which have been formed by response to the emergencies of a small corner of space and time, could possibly comprehend a revelation of the total universe even if it were granted to them. I can understand that we might be given a mystical intuition of the nature of the universe, and this would penetrate to the core of our being, which lies far beneath the level of our consciousness, and would determine our thoughts and actions – indeed, I believe that we must have received such an intuition, for otherwise we would not so often love life when by all logical criteria it is unlovable. But creeds claim to do much more than convey or support mystical intuitions. They pretend to explain the total universe in terms comprehensible to the human intellect, and that pretention seems to me bound to be invalid. I feel this as strongly about the non-Christian and anti-Christian creeds as about the Christian creeds, in so far as they make the statement, which seems to me the lie of lies, that seeks to cut down the growing tree of life before it has borne fruit, 'All is now known.'

I have, as I have said, no faith, in the sense of a store of comforting beliefs. But I have faith in a process, in a particular process that is part of the general process of life, though it is sometimes annulled by it. I find an ultimate value in the efforts of human beings to do more than merely exist, to choose and analyse their experiences and by the findings of that analysis help themselves to further experiences which are of a more pleasurable kind. I use the word pleasurable in its widest sense: to describe such experiences as come from good food and wine, exercise, the physical act of love-making, the practice of a beloved craft or art or science, a happy marriage, the care of children or the sick or the old by those who enjoy it, the service of valid ideas or the administration of worthy institutions or the pursuit of art or science. *Trahit sua quemque voluptas.* By indulgence in these experiences life is made more pleasant from day to day. That is in itself of the first importance. That end would be worthwhile pursuing if no other benefit were obtained. But it also serves the purpose of furnishing each human soul with access to the avenue along which it can advance farthest toward the comprehension and mastery of life. Pleasure is not arbitrary; it is the sign by which the human organization shows that it is performing a function which it finds appropriate to its means and ends. I take it as a prime cause of the present confusion of society that it is too sickly and too doubtful frankly to use pleasure as a test of value.

There is, of course, the objection that man's tastes are so inherently vicious that if pleasure is taken as a standard he would exhaust his vital powers in drunkenness and sexual licence. I do not believe this to be true of humanity as we know it in our civilization. It obviously is true in certain circumstances which prevent the development of alternative amusements. Convincing evidence of that is given in John Morris' anthropological study, *Living with Lepchas*, but the evidence speaks of a restriction of general appetite quite as remarkable as the indulgence of these particular appetites. I have observed human beings for a number of years in the United States and in all countries of Europe, except Russia, Poland, Rumania, and Turkey; and I do not find that dissipations of this sort are their special temptation. The mass of people who drink are found in the groups who, either by reason of extreme wealth or poverty, are cut off from the normal process of exploiting knowledge and capacities; and even of those groups they form an extremely small proportion. There is little evidence to show that sex is a greater danger than alcohol. It is doubtful whether Western men and women have any marked excess of sexual potency over and above what is required in a monogamous relationship. Certainly men and women require a certain amount of sexual intercourse, and in modern times they own to this need, and many insist on satisfying it by unsanctioned means if social and economic barriers stand between them and the sanctioned means; but there are few signs that either men or women want to indulge in sexual intercourse to an extent that is damaging either to themselves or society. Except where the peasantry are so poor that it has to count its daughters as livestock in order to survive, the number of women in any community who become prostitutes is small; and those that do rely for custom chiefly on travellers and men who are obliged to work far from home. There is about as much reason to suppose that mankind is likely to wreck itself by drunkenness and lechery as there is to suppose that it will extinguish itself by vegetarianism, teetotalism, and celibacy.

The fear that pleasure is an unreliable standard because the common man will identify pleasure with debauchery has two sources, neither of which is discreditable. First, there is the recollection of the difficulty found in more elementary stages of society to distract man from concentration on the simpler forms of animal gratification. This is strong in people who have been involved with a deprived proletariat, either as a despised member of that class or as one of the despising *bourgeoisie*. Secondly, there is the exaggerated consciousness of a real twofold difficulty in education. It is certainly not easy to convince young people that the simple and direct pleasures of 'having a good time' will pale before the more complicated pleasures of adult life, which may even involve having quite a bad time. There is no way of giving a pinafored child a certain proof that ultimately it will like many kinds of food and drink far better that an ice-cream soda, or assuring a boy of sixteen that some day he may find working in a tropical hospital just as enjoyable as speeding in an automobile, or a girl of sixteen that some day she may find just as great happiness in looking after several children on small means as she does in dancing. It is also difficult to persuade young people to undergo the preliminary training necessary for them to enjoy adult pleasures, since this is often temporarily painful. The elementary stages of musical education are usually intensely boring, even to those who are best able to profit from it later. On both these sources of fear candour can shine with a helpful light. We need not be afraid that the drunkenness and promiscuity of the slums reveal the common trend of human life if we admit to ourselves that the greater decorum of the *bourgeoisie* is the result not of renunciation, which is indeed not a process we can count upon, but of command over more refined and satisfying means of self-indulgence. The educational difficulty is much graver. It can never be easily solved; if adults admitted to children that they lived for pleasure, of the value of which every child has an intuitive knowledge, instead of for some undefined value which is served by renunciation, children would put much more trust in the good faith of adults and accept their advice about the most useful preparation for life.

It is of paramount importance that these difficulties should be faced and that pleasure should be recognized as a reasonable standard, for certainly chaos establishes itself if we do not. The belief that all higher life is governed by the idea of renunciation poisons our moral life by engendering vanity and egotism. It is actually the case with most of us that we are creatures of limited potency, with hardly enough capacity to carry out the regular routine to fulfill the responsibilities to which we were born. Our problem is to increase our vigour and to respect and aid those among us who are in possession of exceptional vigour, but we are distracted from our attack on it by our pretence that we have already solved a problem of a much more spectacular kind. A man of mediocre gifts, whose task it is to keep stoked the furnace of a moderate-sized dwelling house, is not likely to do it better if he is under the delusion that he has just extinguished a colossal forest fire. It is also actually the case that if we take gratification as our ideal we thereby impose on ourselves a programme of self-restraint; for if we claim that we are under the necessity of learning all that we can about reality, and that we learn most through pleasure, we must also admit that we are under the necessity of hearing what our fellow creatures learn about it and of working out a system by which we all curb our pleasures so that they do not interfere with those of others. If, however, we claim that it is by renunciation that we achieve wisdom, we have no logical reason for feeling any disapproval of conditions that thrust pain and deprivation on others. It is easy thereafter to fall into the depths of humbugging greed and dishonesty, especially in regard to the maintenance of inequitable economic situations. The premises of this philosophy make it possible to gratify all the baser impulses under a cloak of propriety by saying: 'I am a rich man, but I have this and that individual sorrow which keeps me a saved and spiritual man. It is true that the source and extent of my wealth are such that others have to go poor in order that I should have it, but this is a good thing, as it provides them with the barrier between them and their desires which is necessary for salvation.'

This attitude inevitably engenders hatred. Where the inequality of economic conditions is too marked, where a faulty system holds a number of workers on the subsistence line, it becomes necessary for the rich to pretend that the poor are a separate and wicked race, who would certainly be damned if they were not given this opportunity for purification through misery. This is a point of view which was openly expressed in all Western literature during the eighteenth and nineteenth centuries; and though that class at which it is now fashionable to sneer, the intellectuals, have jeered at this hypocrisy till it rarely dares show its face in print, it is repeatedly expressed in the conversation and oratory of the possessing classes.

But indeed we need no further argument in favour of taking pleasure as a standard when we consider the only alternative that faces us. If we do not live for pleasure we will soon find ourselves living for pain. If we do not regard as sacred our own joys and the joys of others, we open the door and let into life the ugliest attribute of the human race, which is cruelty. I believe this vice to be as much of a shame and a doom to humanity as the original sin of the theologians; and I believe it to be the root of all other vices. I do not believe people are cruel because they are greedy; I am sure they invent greed as a pretext for cruelty. I am as sure that the sexual caprice which makes people desert still loving mates or thrust their attentions on those who are offended by them has not its origin in the pure sexual instinct, but is a use made of it by cruelty, seeking an instrument. I take it that cruelty is an early error of the mind, which becomes a confirmed habit before reason can disperse it. Hatred necessarily precedes love in human experience. After the tideless peace of pre-natal existence the child is born into a world of uncomfortable physical experiences and terrifying uncomprehended controls. It must feel that in order to preserve itself it must lay about it, it must beat with its hands, and plot evil against the aggressors. Thus a habit is initiated; thus a fantasy is engendered. It is imagined that it is right to inflict pain, which is given the most intricate and noxious ramifications by early experience. When one inflicts pain on the surrounding world one is punished, one is treated as guilty. This does not rob pain of its majesty; one suffers a greater pain than one inflicted, for punishment is pain, and punishment is acclaimed as good and holy. Is it not a way of salvation to be punished?

The last question the mind, being no fool, transforms quickly into another. If it did not do so, the human race would quickly become extinct, rushing forward to impale itself on expiatory tortures. Out of the instinct for self-preservation, and logically enough, it asks, 'If it is a good and holy thing to be punished, must it not also be a good and holy thing to punish?' It answers that it is; and our earth becomes the hell it is. Thus we human beings plant in ourselves the perennial blossom of cruelty: the conviction that if we hurt other people we are doing good to ourselves and to life in general. It determines the course of all history, the forms of our institutions, the pattern of our lives; and the effect of it in all these spheres is death. It cannot have any other result, since pain is a warning that something is being done to the organism which is inimical to its well-being.

To destroy this cancer of our spirit is our real problem. Since its destruction means the correction of the whole structure of life down to the foundations that were laid when it first became self-conscious, it is a problem which is almost certainly beyond our power ever to solve completely. When we put our hands to this problem we must abandon all hope of success, certainly in our time, possibly in eternity. This is, however, of no importance. Any success achieved against cruelty is in itself absolute. I mean by this that it gives us and those from whom the cruel act has been averted an intense pleasure which could not be increased by a quantitative increase of the success. To pretend that those of us who hate cruelty are martyrs pledged to fighting a hopeless battle is humbug. We are liable to feel great anger and distress and to be put in prison and physically injured by cruel people. But actually we have a great deal more pleasure in our lives than those who pretend that the only problem before us is to curb an imaginary tendency toward intemperance and excess copulation. Perhaps because they are perpetually confronted with evidence disproving their case, since the mass of human beings are sober and continent and nevertheless life is horrible, they are hag-ridden by irritability and intolerance.

I was made aware of the part cruelty plays in the world during my childhood, because I grew up in the shadow of the Dreyfus case. I am of pure Aryan descent. Though naturally I now feel a certain shame in confessing this, I must mention it here to make it quite clear the Dreyfus case was discussed in my home circle with complete detachment. My father had been an army officer, and would have been a great criminal lawyer had he chosen another career, and he could judge both the military and legal aspects of the trial; and my mother was a woman of brilliant understanding and considerable experience of Continental life. They had talked over the case from the beginning, and later they had a special insight into it when the great journalist, G. W. Steevens, with whose family mine was very friendly, was sent to Rennes to report the trial. The earlier stages of the trial took place when I was too young to follow it; but I suppose I absorbed it through the pores, and I certainly remembered its later stages, culminating in the return from Rennes and the rehabilitation of Dreyfus. Therefore I learned early that a people, saddened by defeat and thirsting for a miraculous restorative draught, fancied that it could administer such to itself by the simple process of punishing a man for an offence of which they could not possibly believe him guilty: that is to say, the severest form of punishment conceivable, punishment on a pretext which the victim knows to be unjust.

I confirmed the existence of this human tendency in my youth when I examined certain laws laid down by society for the regulation of the position of the sexes. I realized that the subjection of women serves no purpose whatsoever except to gratify the desire for cruelty both in women and in men. This is obvious in connection with one common phenomenon springing from the sexual instinct. The story of Gretchen in Goethe's *Faust* is its classic example in literature. There are adventures which plainly punish themselves. A girl lives with a man outside marriage, and when she has a child he leaves her without the support of his affection or his money; a woman deserts her husband for a lover who tires of her and deserts her in turn. Such women are obviously far from fortunate. They cannot hope to have as easy or pleasant lives as ordinary women. But society, instead of letting them get on with their imperfect lives as they can, sets about visiting them with every petty annoyance that it can think of, as if they had found out some way of living that is enormously enjoyable and likely to be followed by all women if they are not discouraged by the spectacle of persecution; the reason for this odd behaviour is plain when it is observed that an intoxication, a perversion of pleasure similar to that given by drugs or drink, fills and inflames all the people who take part in these attempts at annoyance. The majority has, in fact, found a minority which it is safe to hurt. Such women are bound to form only a small proportion of the population; the inducements to normal sexual behaviour, the secure possession of a husband and the first claim on his affections and economic resources, are likely to overcome all but the strongest compulsions. Therefore the majority of women who are not as these, and the entire male sex, have here a safe object for their aggressive instincts.

Much incidental suffering follows; but what is even more important is that the public mind has been sidetracked from working out a system of morality by which the genetic interests of the human races are subserved. If you say to a man and woman to-day, 'You must exercise self-control for the sake of your children,' they will instantly see a picture of themselves refraining from having sexual intercourse with some attractive members of the opposite sex, who would probably never look at them in any circumstances; and naturally you will find it hard to gain their sympathy or even their attention while you explain that what you mean is that the time has now come for adults to curb their appetites and make the provision of the goods necessary for the development of sound children a first charge on the economic resources of society, thus buying milk and peace before luxuries and adventure.

But it is important not to make the mistake of supposing that you can make people exchange a sexual morality that serves the interest of cruelty for one that serves the interest of love without imposing real and hideous suffering on them. I reiterate that cruelty is a part of our structure, that naturally we function by it. The proof lies in consideration of another aspect of the feminist movement. All over the world men put women to great inconvenience by pretending that women are as inferior to them in mind and character and social value as they are in muscular strength. I myself used to think this to be a caprice springing from vanity, which could be as easily corrected as a girl's belief that she is not only very beautiful but the most beautiful girl in the world, without any catastrophic results. I am now sure that I was quite wrong.

In the economic depression that befell Europe and America after 1929, many men fell into unemployment and were swept with their wives and families to the brink of starvation; but some men who lost their employment had wives who, by reason of some special talents or aptitude for industries unaffected by the depression, were able to earn wages and support themselves and their husband and children. In any sane world the men in the second group would have been happier than the men in the first. They would realize, sometimes very painfully, that society is wise in at least one of its conventions and that it saves a lot of trouble as a general rule if men go out to work and women stay at home; but they would be glad that a temporary suspension of the general rule had saved themselves and those whom they loved from hardship, and proud that their wives possessed the talent which made this possible. But in fact this was not so. The men of the first group, who had suffered and seen those whom they loved suffer, were damaged far less by their experiences than the men in the second. Many of them were spoiled by them, it would seem for ever. Some fell into infantilism and wanted to remain in a permanent state of dependence; and others formed a deep feeling of resentment against their wives which was sometimes so intense that it led to divorce.

This seems to mean that a large number of men need to believe that the reason that wives do not go out to earn a living is that they cannot. Yet it cannot mean that. A man might sincerely believe that his wife or any woman cannot scale the heights of achievement which have been reached by man: he may doubt that a female Mozart or Shakespeare can exist. But he really cannot sincerely believe that women, who keep the race alive by their competent performance of the tricky jobs of tending babies and the sick, and who undertake a large part of its education, are incapable of reaching the comparatively low standard of capacity demanded by the capitalist system from the mass of its employees. What he needs is to pretend that they could not, and to pretend that even if there were certain women who could, the particular women in his family could not.

This allegation of inferiority, when it is unfounded, amounts to the same sort of cruelty as keeping an animal in a cage too small for it; and it is cruel in the same manner as anti-Semitism, since the victims know themselves undeserving of such pain. But, like anti-Semitism, it fortifies the soul of those who inflict it, so that a man who was deprived of this fortification just at the moment when the economic system had defeated him, really suffered a serious injury of the soul.

The converse can be seen in a society where men have played as virile a part as anywhere in the world.

The Christian men in the East of Europe, who were conquered by the Turks and, largely by the connivance of the Western powers, left in their power for five hundred years, were during all that time starved and misgoverned and despised. They preserved their culture and their courage untainted so that they never let die the knowledge and the hope of freedom, and in the Balkan Wars took back their land and re-established their civilization as if there were no death, as if life was an indestructible condition which nothing could threaten. Living among them, one perceives they are sustained by a certain kind of primitive Christianity, by music, by the subjection of women. There is no reason why the Balkan man should be angry with the Balkan woman – there is no competition between the sexes; she is loving and thrifty, her embroideries put her among the world's great artists. Yet in theory she is regarded as if she were an idiot, unhelpful, a beast that has to be fought back lest it turn dangerous; and in practice she is often treated so. She suffers immensely, but it is plain the suffering has not been wasted. It is so much red blood in the veins of her menfolk.

It may be argued that if a need to inflict cruelty is so inherent in our nature, and its satisfaction such a stimulus to performance, there can be nothing more useless and dangerous than to interfere with it. That is exactly the issue, it seems to me, on which we have to part company with the obvious and convenient if we are to be morally respectable. It is not tolerable that humanity should continue to pay such a price for well-being. Nor is it a simple matter of continuance, for an appetite grows by what it feeds on, and there is no knowing to what hell our developed love of cruelty may lead us before the earth cools and we come to an end. It is not a question of submitting to the subjection of women, and taking that as so much coin to be painfully put down. It might perfectly well happen that some scientific discovery and some change in the environment might put women into a position of power over men, and that women might find it immensely stimulating to develop a theory, and enforce it in practice, that men were happiest if they ran about on all fours with their posteriors painted like mandrils and were never allowed to learn to read. There is no end to the cantrips we may indulge in if we do not eradicate this cruelty from our nature, or to the deterioration of our history that may result; for if cruelty is a stimulus to action, it also determines the quality of our actions.

There are certain general ideas which seem to m
us by the recognition of this cruelty. One is the r
of speech and the arts. We have to scrutiniz⌐
society to judge whether they are cruel or frustr⌐
that purpose we must hear the evidence of all persons a⌐
operation and of all persons qualified by experience or ⌐
speculative gifts to form an interesting opinion on what
operations might be. It is therefore necessary that all classes of m⌐
should be given the fullest opportunity to express themselves without
constraint, not out of admiration for an abstraction, but as a practical
measure toward human survival. It is also necessary that the artist, of
whatsoever kind, should be free to anatomize the spirit, so that we can
comprehend the battlefield that is this life, and which are the troops of
light and which of darkness, and what light may be, and what
darkness. For the essence of our human plight is confusion. Those
who love cruelty dress themselves up as its enemies, and those who
hate it appear to be, and sometimes are, its servants.

This deception is crystallized in its most pictorial, in its most
horribly important form, by the history of Christianity. The spectacle
of the rise of Fascism, and some contact with the Eastern Church,
which is many centuries nearer primitive Christianity than the
Western church, have made it clear to me that the life of Christ should
have been an incomparable blessing to man and a revelation of the
way he must follow if he is not to be a beast, and a failure at that.
Christ was an incarnate denunciation of cruelty. He was sinless, he
was full of love, he was ingenious in devising prescriptions of mercy;
he was what the world needed, he could have taught us how to make
life a perpetual pleasure. Society could find nothing better to do with
him than kill him. Here was a man who could have saved his life if he
had dissimulated his virtue. He unveiled it, knowing that he made
himself a target for man's arrows. Just as a great artist finds the
perfect myth to symbolize the truth he has discovered, that shall sum
it up in a form that is acceptable by the human faculty of attention, so
his crucifixion demonstrated exactly what the assault of cruelty on the
innocent means; and the subsequent services devised by the early
Church commemorated the beauty of the virtue that was slain and the
beastliness shown by the slayer, and reiterated the warning that this
was the kind of crime man was inherently likely to commit unless he
watched himself. There could be no more proper medicine for the
human disease.

ut conventional piety pours as much of the draught as it can down
drain by its attempts to develop a doctrine to account for the
ucifixion of Christ as an atonement for the sins of man instead of a
demonstration of them. These attempts are founded on the primitive
idea of the magical value of sacrifice for propitiating the powers that
be, and they were initiated by St. Paul, out of the legalistic quality of
his mind. They were carried further by the Fathers of the Church, and
given lasting authority by St. Augustine, the first theologian to be
dominated by St. Paul. He was one of the greatest of geniuses and a
most lovable character, but he was also a violent man, in love with
violence and unrepelled by cruelty. He therefore found great pleasure
in imagining a gross drama in which the devil held humanity in his
power by reason of its sins and would have condemned it to death
wholesale had he not killed Christ, after which he could not claim the
blood of humanity since in the divine life of Christ he had been paid so
much more than it owed him. Since God is omnipotent, He is of
course responsible for this whole arrangement, and Augustine admits
that He could have arranged for the redemption of man by other
means, and that He chose this one only because it proved His love for
humanity. In fact, a crime which should have shamed humanity into
virtue is shown to be the contrivance of the highest good, and the
criminals to have served the most mystical and exalted of ends. This
doctrine involves so many absurdities that no church, neither Protestant nor Catholic, has ever formulated it precisely and adopted it. But
vaguely as it is held, it nevertheless has poisoned the Western mind
with the suggestion implied in the word atonement. Cruelty has made
the forces of its chief enemy work in its service.

It is the intellect which performs this perversion, though we are
most familiar with its effects in the emotional sphere, with the
disagreeable substitution of exaltation for the shame and pity we
should feel at the sufferings of Christ on the cross which is indulged in
by all the Western churches. But we see it also directly inscribed on
life by conduct, notably in connection with sex and politics. The
desire of men and women to be cruel to the people who commit
themselves to their mercies in a sexual relationship is gratified by the
existence of at least as many men and women who find it possible and
indeed preferable to love those who treat them ill; and these last are as
much responsible for the evil situations in which they are involved as
those who initiate them. They complain of cruelty, the whole of
literature echoes with their sighs; but they present themselves in such

numbers and so stoutly endure the unendurable that the balance of sexual life, save where it is generously subsidized by nonsexual elements, is on the side of suffering.

This history of people shows a not less discreditable balance sheet. Again and again civilization cancels its own advance; so that it is more often than not a half-forgotten idea instead of a developing theme. This is the consequence of a pervasive weakness in the liberal forces that oppose cruel races or systems of government. Their policy is unworthy of their intellectual level, they envelop themselves in organizations which lead to dissension and betrayal, and above all they do not use the full energy that must be at the disposal of such a quantity of persons of such quality. The curious failure of European liberals to stiffen their opposition to militarist tyranny after the Great War of 1914 is typical of a score of passages in the Christian era; such as the frivolity with which the Christian European powers refused to unite against the invading Turks when they came out of Asia.

In the sexual and political spheres alike these defeats are due to the refusal to recognize pleasure as the supreme value in human life. This refusal leaves man to indulge in some of his characteristically false logic. His mind, which is quite inadequate for the purpose of mastering his environment and therefore always oversimplifies, sees the universe in antitheses, in dichotomies. He says, foolishly enough, for one cannot cut into clean halves two substances that pass into each other by insensible gradation, that there is light and darkness, life and death, pleasure and pain. He feels a need to identify these antitheses one with another, and since he is not allowed to make the obvious identification between pleasure and life and light, which would be rough indeed but sound enough save for the most crude and diseased character, he comes to the conclusion that the universe is a queerer place than he thought it, and he agrees with the cruel that life and light are pain. But there is that in all the more decent sorts of human beings which warns them that it is a filthy thing to inflict pain, and therefore all that are most likely to give themselves that warning and take it are likely to put themselves in the position of those on whom pain is inflicted; to be a beaten wife, a cheated husband, is better than being a bullying husband, an idle and spendthrift wife; to be put into a concentration camp is better than to put others into it. This must inevitably happen unless the emphasis is transferred to pleasure. Then only can a good man feel himself at ease in happiness with an unmalignant partner, and in victory over a bad man; then only will the human species have a chance to practise some other art than suicide, and creation oust nothingness.

To live by this philosophy is more difficult than following the old. Pain is always at hand in some form or other, but pleasure is harder to find; and these antitheses are protean and treacherous, always pretending to be one another. Birth control, for example, is a means of pleasure for women in certain circumstances: it enables them not to have more children than they can feed and clothe and adequately love. In other circumstances it can be the means of preventing them from knowing pleasure: it can enable a masculinist society to deny women the right to have any children at all, and keep them as starved and sterile producers and consumers of worthless goods in large towns, and in this second form it affects to make the same offer of freedom as the first, though in fact it enjoins slavery. But more dangerous than the protean nature of environment is the protean nature of our own souls, that constantly avails itself of these changes to pursue its own passion under cover.

It is because of the ineradicable persistence of cruelty in the human species, which may be incorrigible, that I should never be saddened to be warned of its passing. I can imagine no better news than to hear that there had emerged from the South American forest or the Australian desert specimens of a new species which would, by reason of some new organ or adaptation of an organ, be able to dominate man as man has dominated the other animals. They might, particularly if their reproductive systems were differently planned, be less morbid. Our lives would seem more tolerable and more honourable if we could know ourselves a transitional form, superseding what was worse and being superseded by what was better. Not that I feel our lives to be entirely intolerable and dishonourable. The living philosophy which really sustains us, which is our basic nourishment, more than any finding of the mind, is simply the sensation of life, exquisite when it is not painful.